The KITCHEN TABLE *Cookbook*

The
KITCHEN TABLE
Cookbook

MOIRA SANDERS

whitecap

For Alan, Gavin and Ellen ... And especially Oscar.

The following recipes and excerpts have been previously published and used with permission: Chewy White and Dark Chocolate Chunk Cookies (page 229) was previously published as as "Chocolate Chip Cookies" in *Sugar*, by Anna Olson, Whitecap Books, 2004. "A pudding as comforting as an old teddy bear," (page 277) is from *Ripe: A cook in the orchard*, by Nigel Slater, Ten Speed Press, 2010. "Chicken Soup with Rice" (page 49) is from *Chicken Soup with Rice: A Book of Months*, by Maurice Sendak, Harper Collins, 1962 (reprinted in 1991).

EDITOR: Jeffrey Bryan
DESIGNER: Michelle Furbacher
PROOFREADER: Patrick Geraghty
FOOD PHOTOGRAPHY: Mike McColl
ADDITIONAL PHOTOGRAPHY: Moira Sanders

Printed in Canada

Library and Archives Canada Cataloguing in Publication

Sanders, Moira, 1972-, author
  The kitchen table cookbook / by Moira Sanders.

ISBN: 978-1-77050-228-4 (pbk.)

   1. Cooking. 2. Cookbooks. I. Title.

TX714.S3253 2014   641.5   C2014-903228-5

The publisher acknowledges the financial support of the Government of Canada through the Canada Book Fund (CBF) and the Province of British Columbia through the Book Publishing Tax Credit.

14 15 16 17 5 4 3 2 1

Contents

Introduction *1*

Weekday Breakfasts *5*

Weekend Brunches *25*

On-the-Go Lunches *43*

Staying-Put Lunches *59*

Snacks and Treats *77*

Starters *95*

Sides *109*

Weeknight Suppers *127*

Weekend Dinners *151*

Everyday Desserts *173*

Special-Occasion Desserts *193*

Baking Contest Entries *219*

Pantry and Preserves *231*

Drinks *255*

Odds and Ends *269*

My Favourite Cookbooks *277*

Menu Ideas *280*

A Big Thank You . . . *282*

Index *283*

INTRODUCTION

Y ou have in front of you a collection of recipes that have been tried, tweaked, savoured, passed on and enjoyed again and again. If you had no other resource for recipes, you could have all your bases covered for feeding yourself and your family in a delicious manner twelve months of the year. I generally focus on eating local, seasonal and real food, and moderation is the umbrella that everything falls under. Along with the recipes, you'll find yourself making paints, entering your baking and preserves at a local fair, cooking away from home (who's up for some camping?), and investigating your own neighbourhood for the best local food you can find.

Before there was *The Kitchen Table Cookbook*, there was *The Harrow Fair Cookbook*. Published in 2010, *The Harrow Fair Cookbook* was written by myself, my sister Lori Elstone and our cousin Beth Goslin Maloney. It highlighted the agricultural fair in our hometown of Harrow, Ontario and became a Canadian bestseller. It also won a silver medal at the Cuisine Canada Cookbook Awards. So many people have told us that it is a cookbook they actually use over and over again—one of the best compliments that a cookbook author can get, if you ask me. With *The Kitchen Table Cookbook*, I've compiled a new collection of recipes for people to use over and over again. It's a book for anyone who wants to eat great food at home, on the go and everywhere in-between.

Before I ever considered having a family, I became a Red Seal chef. I worked my way from Ontario to British Columbia to the countryside of central France, eventually landing back in small-town Ontario, where I hung up my chef's coat and really started cooking for some picky "customers"! Over the last 12 years I've spent lots of time cooking for my family, researching and testing recipes and eventually writing *The Harrow Fair Cookbook*. Nowadays I teach cooking classes, write articles and read cookbooks, new and old. You see, I'm really a cookbook girl at heart (see a list of my favourites on page 277) and all it takes to make me happy is a hot cup of tea, an interesting cookbook and a comfortable place to sit. Oh yes, and delicious food.

If there is one thing that I want to teach my kids before they leave the nest, it has got to be how to eat and cook. Our house sees a fair bit of traffic with our kids' friends from school and around the neighbourhood. I've realized that a lot of kids have a different idea of what real, everyday food is. And I'm not talking about anything outrageous—just simple, delicious meals with the ability to nurture a family. Although this book is written from the point of view of having a young family, I believe these recipes and stories are just as relevant for people in all stages of their lives. You never know when you may inspire a young person (neighbour, grand-child, nephew or niece, etc.) to enjoy the art of eating well, trying a new food or cooking something for the first time.

. . . .

LOCAL, SEASONAL, REAL

LOCAL FOOD You've probably noticed that every year it seems to be increasingly easier to find local ingredients. Farmers' markets, roadside stands and Community Supported Agriculture farms are all flourishing as people look for a way to eat what is grown close to home. A CSA farm is a wonderful way to eat locally and support the farmers who are working hard to make that possible. Here's how it works: A farm will sell veggie shares to the public before the season starts. The money that is generated helps the farm purchase seeds and supplies for the coming season. Customers then become share members and receive weekly or bi-weekly boxes of vegetables and fruit throughout the growing season. My family have been members of Cooper's CSA Farm, giving us access to veggie shares; beef, pork and poultry shares; and egg shares. As a member of the CSA farm, we are able to wander around their property, enjoying the animals and the ambience of a working farm, as well as unlimited access to their popular corn maze every fall. There are CSA farms all across Canada now and I highly recommend looking into joining one.

SEASONAL FOOD If you are eating locally, it's a given that you are eating seasonally. However, during the coldest months of the year, when farmers are taking a well-deserved break, I find myself in grocery store aisles more often. Eating seasonally means making conscious decisions to eat what is naturally available at certain times of the year or squirreling away enough during the peak growing time that you've got lots in the freezer to get you through the winter. There is nothing I like better than seeing my freezer and canning cupboard full in November and bare in June.

REAL FOOD With the tremendous amount of packaged foods and fast foods to be had these days, is it at all surprising that families are eating less real food and relying more on processed foods? Real food doesn't have to take hours to prepare but it does have to be made with real ingredients. Even I get tempted to cut corners by ordering take-out or eating something out of a box. I don't know anyone that's perfect! But by making a concerted effort to cook real food at home most of the time, you're doing yourself and your family a huge favour.

BAKING CONTESTS

Over the last several years, I have become a baking contest devotee. Local agricultural fairs are a great place to start looking for a contest to enter. I wouldn't consider entering something like a running race, but putting one of my pies up against other competitors' pies is something that I can get excited about!

The first ribbon I won was second place for a pumpkin pie. I entered it without realizing that in order to collect the $20 prize, I had to bake another pie and give it to the family that sponsored the category. I was so thrilled to have won a ribbon, I barely minded having to drive the four hours back to my hometown to deliver the mandatory pie. I am much more careful to read through the prize guides these days. For a list of suggestions on how to put your best foot forward in a baking contest, see page 220.

EATING WHEREVER YOU MAY BE

There seems to be no end to the list of activities that Canadians find themselves doing throughout the year. I have never participated in an activity that wasn't greatly improved by having good food along for the ride. Road trips, ski weekends, baseball tournaments, you name it! In order to make the most of your meals away from home, you'll need access to a grill or a hot plate or two (check out Two-Burner Raspberry Jam, page 243), a large cooler, individual storage containers for prepared ingredients (for chopped veggies, etc.), well-insulated beverage containers, water bottles and ice packs. With these basics, you can cook, carry and store everything you'll need for a weekend's worth of meals. Of course you can get a lot fancier than that but it can certainly be kept very simple. There are lots of recipes in this book that are suitable for outdoor, on-the-go cooking too!

FOOD & FAMILY

It's my opinion that if you pare away the all busyness and unnecessary stresses that don't really matter all that much in the first place, you are left with a handful of things that really count. Food and family are two of those things, and it is my hope that this cookbook will inspire you to focus on what makes life so delicious.

Weekday Breakfasts

Ginger Quinoa Granola   6

Cherry Crumble Oatmeal   8

Sweet Breakfast Custards   9

French Crumpets   11

Cinnamon Butter on Toast   12

Veggie Cream Cheese on Bagels   13

Carrot-Ginger Muffins   14

Strawberry Oatmeal Muffins   16

Buttermilk Pancakes   19

Egg Cups and Toast Shapes   20

Egg-in-the Hole   22

Shirred Eggs with Maple Bacon   23

GINGER QUINOA GRANOLA

Makes 8 cups (2 L)

There is a certain Canadian cereal that really caused a stir when it came out, at least with my kids. The brand Holy Crap (tee hee!) was something that we had to try at least once and I've purchased several bags since. The combination of chia seeds and hemp hearts are what inspired this granola combination, two ingredients that are more or less widely available now (see sidebar). This granola is full of good-for-you ingredients, including quinoa flakes, which come together with little bursts of spicy ginger.

4 cups (1 L) quinoa flakes

1 cup (250 mL) coarsely chopped
   walnuts

½ cup (125 mL) pumpkin seeds

½ cup (125 mL) chia seeds

½ cup (125 mL) hemp hearts

⅔ cup (160 mL) grape seed oil

⅔ cup (160 mL) honey

1 tsp (5 mL) ground ginger

½ cup (125 mL) finely chopped
   candied ginger

PREHEAT THE OVEN to 350°F (175°C). Line a large baking sheet with parchment paper.

Toss the quinoa, walnuts, pumpkin seeds, chia seeds and hemp hearts in a large bowl. Warm the oil, honey and ground ginger in a small saucepan over low heat until the ingredients are smooth. Pour over the dry ingredients and stir well.

Spread the mixture on the prepared pan. Bake for 20 minutes, stirring once or twice. Continue baking for another 5–10 minutes, until the granola starts to turn golden brown. Remove from the oven and add the candied ginger. Allow the granola to cool on the baking sheet completely before storing.

Storage: Store the granola in an airtight container for up to 1 month.

QUINOA FLAKES Quinoa flakes are made by pressing grains of quinoa, which makes the cooking time much shorter than with regular quinoa. Like regular quinoa, the flakes are high in protein and gluten-free. Quinoa flakes are often used as a substitute for rolled oats.

HEMP HEARTS Known as a "superfood", hemp hearts are found inside the shell of hemp seeds and contain a highly concentrated balance of proteins, fats, vitamins and enzymes.

CHIA SEEDS Chia seeds are high in omega-3 fats, protein, fibre and antioxidants. And they make those cute chia pets as well!

My favourite way to eat granola is with plain whole-milk yogurt and a drizzle of honey. Making your own yogurt is a habit that you can feel good about. I have a Euro Cuisine Yogurt Maker and it's child's play to make fresh yogurt with high quality organic milk. For fruity yogurts, follow the manufacturer's directions for your yogurt maker and add 1 or 2 tsp (5–10 mL) of Strawberry-Vanilla Freezer Jam (page 234) or Peach Freezer Jam (page 239) to the bottom of each jar before you add the milk.

· ·

CHERRY CRUMBLE OATMEAL

Serves 4–6

A hot bowl of oatmeal always makes me nostalgic for cold-weather breakfasts around my family's kitchen table. By adding dried cherries, cinnamon and walnuts to the mix, the smell of this oatmeal wafting through the house will have everyone making a beeline for the kitchen.

4 cups (1 L) water	¼ cup (60 mL) butter
1 cup (250 mL) steel-cut oatmeal	½ cup (125 mL) finely chopped
½ cup (125 mL) dried cherries	walnuts
½ tsp (2.5 mL) ground cinnamon	cream or milk, for serving
¼ cup (60 mL) brown sugar	

BRING THE WATER to a boil in a large saucepan. Add the oatmeal, dried cherries and cinnamon and return the mixture to a boil. Lower the heat and simmer for about 30 minutes, or until the oatmeal has softened and thickened.

Remove the oatmeal from the heat and stir in the brown sugar, butter and walnuts. Serve hot, with cream or milk if desired.

Storage: Refrigerate leftover oatmeal in an airtight container. To reheat the oatmeal, place in a small saucepan with a splash of water and warm over low heat.

SWEET BREAKFAST CUSTARDS

Serves 6

If there was a custard fan club, I'd most likely be el presidente. *I don't believe there is ever a wrong time of the day for the comforting combination of sweetened eggs and milk, and this recipe proves my point. These make excellent quick breakfasts or easy after-school snacks.*

3 large eggs	3 cups (750 mL) milk
⅓ cup (80 mL) honey	1 tsp (5 mL) pure vanilla extract

PREHEAT THE OVEN to 300°F (150°C). Place 6 individual ramekins in a 9- × 13-inch (23 × 33 cm) baking dish. Set aside until needed.

Whisk the eggs and honey together in a large bowl, preferably with a spout. Add the milk and vanilla extract to the egg mixture and whisk until thoroughly incorporated.

Pour the mixture into the ramekins. Pour hot water into the baking dish until it comes about halfway up the sides of the ramekins. Place the baking dish in the oven and bake for 1 hour and 15 minutes.

Remove the baking dish from the oven and remove the ramekins to cool. Serve warm or let cool, cover and refrigerate until needed.

Storage: The custards will keep, covered, in the refrigerator for up to 3 days.

VARIATIONS Try adding 1 Tbsp (15 mL) of your favourite fibre cereal, or 1 tsp (5 mL) of your favourite jam to the bottom of each ramekin before adding the custard mixture.

FRENCH CRUMPETS

Serves 2–3

The photographer of this book, Mike McColl, a seasoned chef in his own right, wasn't sure what to make of this recipe before he tried it. Afterwards, this was one of the recipes that he went home and made for his family immediately. This is the best possible use of store-bought crumpets that I know of. Think French toast with lots of nooks and crannies. I love breakfast.

FOR THE HONEYCOMB BUTTER

4 oz (120 g) honeycomb

¼ cup (60 mL) butter, at room temperature

FOR THE FRENCH CRUMPETS

4 eggs

½ cup (125 mL) milk

1 tsp (5 mL) granulated sugar

1 tsp (5 mL) pure vanilla extract

6 fresh crumpets (1 package)

1 Tbsp (15 mL) butter

1 Tbsp (15 mL) grape seed oil

FOR THE HONEYCOMB BUTTER: Place the honeycomb and the butter into the bowl of a stand mixer fitted with the paddle attachment. Blend together on medium speed until the honeycomb has broken down and becomes somewhat uniform in the butter. Place the butter into a small dish and set aside until needed.

FOR THE FRENCH CRUMPETS: Whisk the eggs, milk, sugar and vanilla together in a large bowl. Soak the crumpets in the bowl for at least 10 minutes, flipping and turning them so that each crumpet has a turn in the custard mixture.

Heat the butter and grape seed oil in a large cast-iron skillet over medium heat. Add the crumpets to the pan (in batches if necessary) and cook for 2–3 minutes per side, until the crumpets are golden brown and the custard has set inside of the crumpets. Remove from the pan and serve with the honeycomb butter or maple syrup.

Eating honeycomb may seem old-fashioned but it's actually becoming popular again. It's the most unprocessed method of harvesting honey and is quite nutritious. Once it's blended together with the butter and served on the hot crumpets, it's perfection. If you don't have honeycomb or you're still not a convert, substitute ¼ cup (60 mL) pure honey and continue with the recipe.

CINNAMON BUTTER ON TOAST

Makes ½ cup (125 mL) cinnamon butter

This is probably more of a memory gleaned from school mornings and running to catch the bus than an actual recipe, but I think it's worth including. In a recipe this simple, it's the quality of the ingredients that really make it shine. Good butter, fresh dark brown sugar and Vietnamese cinnamon are a good place to start.

½ cup (125 mL) butter, at room temperature
½ cup (125 mL) brown sugar

1 Tbsp (15 mL) ground cinnamon, plus more for extra sprinkling
good quality artisan-style crusty bread

COMBINE THE BUTTER, brown sugar and cinnamon in the bowl of a stand mixer fitted with the paddle attachment. Mix together on medium speed for 1 minute.

To make cinnamon toast, toast the bread to your liking. Spread a generous amount of the cinnamon butter on the toast. Sprinkle with extra cinnamon, if desired. Serve immediately.

Storage: Store the cinnamon butter at room temperature in an airtight container for up to 1 week.

VEGGIE CREAM CHEESE ON BAGELS

Makes 1½ cups (375 mL)

My family are not thrilled with the idea of veggies for breakfast. However, mixed with cream cheese and spread on Montreal-style bagels—well that's another story altogether.

8 oz (225 g) cream cheese, at room temperature

¾ cup (185 mL) grated carrots

½ cup (125 mL) finely chopped celery

1 Tbsp (15 mL) finely chopped red onion

1 Tbsp (15 mL) apple cider vinegar

¼ tsp (1 mL) fine sea salt

pinch freshly ground black pepper

good-quality bagels, preferrably Montreal-style

WHIP THE CREAM cheese in the work bowl of a stand mixer fitted with the paddle attachment. Add the remaining ingredients and beat until everything is incorporated. Taste for seasoning. Spread on hot toasted bagels.

Storage: Store leftover veggie cream cheese in an airtight container for up to 3 days.

Montreal-style bagels are smaller, denser and sweeter than their New York-style cousins that most people are familiar with. The sweetness comes from the addition of honey to the dough as well as to the water they are boiled in. Bagels from Montreal are traditionally baked in wood-fired ovens.

CARROT-GINGER MUFFINS

Makes 12 muffins

I was once a judge at a local baking contest that had a carrot theme. I was pleasantly surprised at the variety of carrot baking items that were entered that evening. Carrot pie, anyone?

My carrot muffins are a little more mainstream, but with this recipe I've included one of my favourite flavour combinations—the triple ginger combo: fresh, ground and candied. If you are missing one of these elements, it's not a problem to omit one and still have a great muffin.

2 cups (500 mL) all-purpose flour

2 tsp (10 mL) baking powder

1 tsp (5 mL) ground ginger

½ tsp (2.5 mL) ground cinnamon

½ tsp (2.5 mL) fine sea salt

¾ cup (185 mL) brown sugar

⅔ cup (160 mL) grape seed oil (or other vegetable oil)

2 eggs

2 tsp (10 mL) finely grated fresh ginger

1½ cups (375 mL) grated carrot

1½ cups (375 mL) mashed bananas

½ cup (125 mL) finely chopped candied ginger

HEAT THE OVEN to 350°F (175°C). Line a standard 12-cup muffin pan with paper muffin cups.

Whisk the flour, baking powder, ground ginger, cinnamon and sea salt in a medium bowl. Set aside.

Mix the brown sugar and oil in the bowl of a stand mixer fitted with the paddle attachment. Beat in the eggs, one at a time, with the mixer on low speed. Add the grated ginger.

Add the flour mixture to the egg mixture and mix until combined. Add the grated carrots, mashed bananas and candied ginger and mix gently.

Divide the batter evenly into the muffin cups. Bake for about 30 minutes, or until a toothpick inserted into the centre of the muffin comes out clean.

Cool for 10 minutes before serving.

Storage: These muffins are at their best the day they are made.

Purchase the freshest candied ginger you can find and then store it in an airtight container.

On busy mornings, it's still possible to make a quick batch of muffins. That's what I like about muffin recipes that call for oil instead of butter. You may not always have butter at room temperature, but oil is always ready to go.

STRAWBERRY OATMEAL MUFFINS

Makes 12 muffins

My friend Susan spends her summers on the shores of Prince Edward Island in a place called Tea Hill. This is a muffin that she makes at her family's cottage while everyone else is happily sleeping. I can picture her in a beach chair while the muffins are baking, enjoying a cup of coffee and taking in the view.

2 cups (500 mL) fresh strawberries

1½ cups (375 mL) all-purpose flour

½ cup (125 mL) quick-cooking oatmeal

1 tsp (5 mL) baking powder

1 tsp (5 mL) baking soda

¾ tsp (4 mL) fine sea salt

⅔ cup (160 mL) brown sugar, plus more for sprinkling

⅓ cup (80 mL) grape seed oil

2 eggs

1 cup (250 mL) buttermilk

PREHEAT THE OVEN to 350°F (175°C). Line a standard 12-cup muffin pan with paper muffin cups.

Cut 12 slices of strawberries and reserve to place on the top of each muffin. Halve or quarter the remaining strawberries, depending on how large they are.

Whisk the flour, oatmeal, baking powder, baking soda and salt in a medium bowl. Set aside.

Mix the brown sugar and oil in the bowl of a stand mixer fitted with the paddle attachment. Beat in the eggs, one at a time, with the mixer on low speed.

Combine the flour mixture, egg mixture and buttermilk in parts, alternating between each one. Mix until combined. Add the strawberries (not the ones reserved for the tops) and mix gently.

Divide the batter evenly into the muffin cups. Place a strawberry slice on the top of each muffin. Bake for about 30 minutes, or until a toothpick inserted into the centre of the muffin comes out clean.

Cool for 10 minutes before serving.

Storage: These muffins are at their best the day they are made.

BUTTERMILK PANCAKES

Makes about 12 pancakes

The biggest hurdle for families wanting to enjoy a hot breakfast is TIME. Put together this pancake mix in advance and you'll not only have time to make buttermilk pancakes, you'll get lunches made and even have a few minutes to drink your coffee. These pancakes will keep your family going 'til lunch, or at least until morning recess.

1 cup (250 mL) Homemade Pancake Mix	1 egg
1½ cups (375 mL) buttermilk	2 Tbsp (30 mL) melted butter, divided
	2 Tbsp (30 mL) grape seed oil

COMBINE THE PANCAKE mix, buttermilk, egg and 1 Tbsp (15 mL) melted butter in a large bowl and stir until combined. Do not over mix.

Melt the remaining 1 Tbsp (15 mL) of butter and grape seed oil in a large cast-iron skillet. Spoon about a ¼ cup (60 mL) of batter into the pan for each pancake. Cook until bubbles on the surface of the pancake start to pop. Flip the pancakes and continue cooking until both sides are golden brown.

Serve immediately with warm maple syrup, your favourite jam or Honeycomb Butter (page 11).

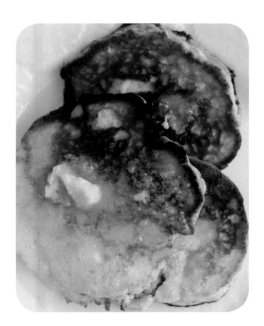

HOMEMADE PANCAKE MIX

Makes about 8 cups (2 L)

7 cups (1.75 L) all-purpose flour
½ cup (125 mL) granulated sugar
½ cup (125 mL) baking powder
2 Tbsp (30 mL) baking soda
1 Tbsp (15 mL) fine sea salt

SIFT ALL OF the ingredients together in a large bowl.

Storage: Store in an airtight container for up to 6 months.

EGG CUPS AND TOAST SHAPES

Serves 4

Boiled eggs are super easy but the timing can sometimes trip people up. I guess that's why so many kitchen timers are in the shape of eggs. I've given you my fool-proof method for boiled eggs that will have a soft to medium done yolk, perfect for dipping your toast into.

My friend Beth always cuts her twin girls' toast into shapes using cookie cutters, a method she has coined "toaster art." What a fun way to start the day!

8 eggs	pinch fine sea salt
8 slices of your favourite bread	pinch freshly ground black pepper
butter	

BRING A SMALL pot of water to a boil. Lower the eggs into the boiling water with a slotted spoon and reduce the heat to medium. Simmer for 5 minutes for a white that is cooked and a yolk that is still soft and spreadable.

While the eggs are cooking, toast the bread. Cut shapes out of the toast using a sharp cookie cutter. Butter the toast shapes.

Run the eggs under cold water for about 30 seconds to stop the cooking. Place the eggs into egg cups and cut the tops off the eggs with a sharp knife. Sprinkle with a pinch of salt and pepper, if desired. Serve immediately with the toast shapes.

EGG-IN-THE-HOLE

Serves 4

My mom used to call this "toad-in-the-hole." I love the name but in recent years I realized that a true "toad-in-the-hole" is actually sausages baked in a Yorkshire pudding batter, an old British concoction. Whatever name you use, this is a quick, hot breakfast and is very satisfying.

8 slices of your favourite bread

butter, as desired

8 eggs

pinch fine sea salt

pinch freshly ground black pepper

HEAT A CAST-IRON skillet over medium heat. Butter both sides of the bread slices. Cut a hole in the middle of each slice of bread with a round cookie cutter, about 2 inches (5 cm) in diameter.

Place the buttered bread and the circles into the warm pan. Crack an egg into the holes and sprinkle with salt and pepper. Cook until the toast is golden brown and the egg is cooked on one side, about 2 minutes. Flip the bread over and continue cooking for another 2 minutes or until that side of the bread is golden brown and the egg is done to your liking. I like mine with a slightly runny yolk.

Transfer the eggs-in-the-holes to plates and serve immediately with the toast circles.

SHIRRED EGGS WITH MAPLE BACON

Serves 4

Shirred eggs are simply eggs and a little cream, baked in the oven. They are a quick, low maintenance breakfast, but by adding cheddar cheese and green onions they become special enough for company—even your mother-in-law will love them! Serve with hot buttered toasted baguettes and Maple Bacon. These are also delicious for a light lunch.

soft butter, for buttering 8 ramekins	¼ cup (60 mL) finely chopped green onions
8 eggs	½ cup (125 mL) grated sharp cheddar cheese
fine sea salt	
freshly ground black pepper	½ cup (125 mL) whipping cream

PREHEAT THE OVEN to 350°F (175°C). Butter 8 ramekins and place the ramekins on a baking sheet.

Crack an egg into each of the ramekins. Sprinkle each egg with a pinch of salt and pepper. Divide the green onions and cheddar cheese among the 8 ramekins. Drizzle each ramekin with 1 Tbsp (15 mL) whipping cream.

Bake in the oven for about 10 minutes, keeping an eye on the eggs so that they don't overcook. Serve immediately with hot toast and Maple Bacon.

MAPLE BACON

Serves 4

Yes, I know that it's possible to buy maple bacon at the grocery store. No, I don't buy it. This is easy enough to make and it's the real deal.

1 lb (500 g) good-quality bacon
½ cup (125 mL) real maple syrup

PREHEAT THE OVEN to 375°F (190°C). Line a large baking sheet with parchment paper.

Lay the bacon slices in a single layer on the baking sheet. Brush each bacon slice with maple syrup, using about half of the amount.

Bake in the oven for about 10 minutes. Turn the bacon and brush the rest of the maple syrup on this side. Return to the oven and bake for another 10 minutes or until the bacon starts to darken and crisp up (or cook to your liking). Serve warm.

Weekend Brunches

Puffy Apple Pancake   *26*

Cheddar and Red Onion Biscuits   *27*

White Chocolate Apricot Scones   *29*

Old-Fashioned Sour Cream Coffee Cake   *30*

Sweet Potato and Zucchini Bread   *32*

Jammy Bread Pudding   *33*

Overnight Pumpkin Waffles   *34*

Roasted Peameal Bacon   *36*

Turkey Sausage Patties   *37*

Cheesy Potato Casserole with Grilled Sausages   *38*

Asparagus and Ham Quiche   *41*

PUFFY APPLE PANCAKE

Serves 4

Caramelized apples hidden in a thin pancake batter that puffs dramatically in the oven as it bakes? Sounds like the perfect autumn breakfast to me! This recipe takes all of 20 minutes from start to finish, making it a great choice for those of us that wake up with breakfast on our mind.

¼ cup (60 mL) butter	⅓ cup (80 mL) milk
1 apple, peeled, cored and thinly sliced	⅓ cup (80 mL) whipping cream
	2 eggs
1½ Tbsp (22.5 mL) granulated sugar	¼ tsp (1 mL) ground cinnamon
½ cup (125 mL) all-purpose flour	icing sugar

PREHEAT THE OVEN to 450°F (230°C).

Place a large 10-inch (25 cm) cast-iron skillet over medium heat. Melt the butter and add the sliced apple pieces. Sprinkle with sugar and cook the apples until softened and starting to caramelize, about 5 minutes.

While the apples are cooking, whisk together the flour, milk, cream, eggs and cinnamon until smooth.

Add the batter to the pan with the apples and place immediately in the oven. Cook for about 12–15 minutes. Remove from the oven, sift a bit of icing sugar on top and cut into 4 wedges. Serve immediately.

CHEDDAR AND RED ONION BISCUITS

Makes 12 biscuits

These are the most savoury, taste-bud tempting biscuits ever. Here they are in the Weekend Brunch chapter, but they would have been welcomed with open arms in several other chapters of this book. In other words, no matter the time of day, make these your go-to biscuits.

2 cups (500 mL) all-purpose flour

1 Tbsp (15 mL) baking powder

2 tsp (10 mL) granulated sugar

1 tsp (5 mL) fine sea salt

½ tsp (2.5 mL) baking soda

¼ cup (60 mL) cold butter, cut into
  small cubes

½ cup (125 mL) finely diced cheddar
  cheese

¼ cup (60 mL) finely diced red onion

1½ cups (375 mL) buttermilk

2 Tbsp (30 mL) melted butter

PREHEAT THE OVEN to 400°F (200°C). Butter a 9-inch (23 cm) round cake pan and set aside until needed.

Place the flour, baking powder, sugar, salt and baking soda in the work bowl of a stand mixer fitted with the paddle attachment. Add the cold butter and mix for about 30 seconds until the butter has become mostly incorporated. Add the cheese and red onion and mix until combined. Pour the buttermilk into the biscuit mixture with the mixer on low speed and mix until combined.

Scoop the dough out into ¼ cup (60 mL) portions. Arrange the dough portions in the prepared pan, spacing them evenly apart. Brush with the melted butter.

Bake for 20–25 minutes or until the biscuits are golden on top. Remove from the oven and let cool for a few minutes before serving.

Storage: These biscuits are best eaten the day they are made.

WHITE CHOCOLATE APRICOT SCONES

Makes about 24 scones

Scones hold a special place in the heart of my friend Brenda. Her parents came to Canada in the 1960's, leaving England and all of their family behind to begin a new life. They started their own bakery in the small town of Goderich, Ontario, and you can bet that scones were on the menu. I'm sure Brenda would love a batch of these special scones but for her, a plain scone with clotted cream and jam evokes a sense of family history and a way to share memories with her own family today.

I've made more than my share of scones over the years. My love affair with baking scones started in the wee hours of the morning on my first day selling baked goods at our local farmers' market. Cheddar-dill and maple-oatmeal were the flavours and they were the first items to sell out, even though they had been a last-minute addition. People would walk away with their scones and within minutes they were coming back with the question, "Will you be here next week?"

4 cups (1 L) all-purpose flour	5 large eggs, divided
2 Tbsp (30 mL) granulated sugar, plus more for sprinkling	1 cup (250 mL) whipping cream
2 Tbsp (30 mL) baking powder	1 cup (250 mL) chopped dried apricots
1 tsp (5 mL) fine sea salt	¾ cup (185 mL) chopped white chocolate
1½ cups (375 mL) cold butter, diced into small pieces	2 Tbsp (30 mL) milk

PREHEAT THE OVEN to 400°F (200°C). Line a large baking sheet with parchment paper.

Combine the flour, sugar, baking powder and salt in the bowl of a stand mixer fitted with the paddle attachment. Blend in the cold butter at the lowest speed and mix until the butter is in pea-sized pieces.

In a separate bowl, combine 4 eggs and whipping cream and quickly add them to the flour and butter mixture. Combine until just blended. Add the dried apricots and white chocolate and mix quickly. The dough may be a bit sticky.

Dump the dough out onto a lightly floured surface. Roll out the dough to about a 1-inch (2.5 cm) thickness. You should see little lumps of butter in the dough. Cut out the dough into 2-inch (5 cm) circles. Reroll the scraps but don't overwork the dough too much. Place on the prepared baking sheet.

Combine the remaining egg with the milk and brush the tops of the scones with the egg wash. Sprinkle with granulated sugar and bake for 18–20 minutes, until the scones start to turn golden. Serve warm.

Storage: Scones are at their best the day they are made.

OLD-FASHIONED SOUR CREAM COFFEE CAKE

Serves 12

I had an after-school job washing hair at Maria's Hair Villa, a busy hair salon in Harrow, Ontario. Those were the days of roller sets, and the ladies would come in weekly to have their hair done. While I had them in the shampoo chair, inevitably we would talk recipes. This coffee cake was inspired by a recipe given to me by one of our regulars who was a home economics professor at the University of Windsor. She was one of many wonderful bakers that used to bring goodies and share their recipes with me. I miss the days, pre-internet, when sharing a recipe meant a hand-written file card and a signature at the bottom.

TOPPING

½ cup (125 mL) brown sugar

½ cup (125 mL) pecans, finely
  chopped

2 tsp (10 mL) ground cinnamon

1 tsp (5 mL) ground nutmeg

CAKE BATTER

2½ cups (625 mL) all-purpose flour

2 tsp (10 mL) baking powder

1 tsp (5 mL) baking soda

½ tsp (2.5 mL) fine sea salt

¾ cup (185 mL) butter, at room
  temperature

1½ cups (375 mL) brown sugar

3 eggs

2 tsp (10 mL) pure vanilla extract

2 cups (500 mL) sour cream

PREHEAT THE OVEN to 350°F (175°C). Butter a Bundt pan or tube pan generously and set aside until needed.

For the topping, mix the brown sugar, chopped pecans, cinnamon and nutmeg in a small bowl. Set aside until needed.

Whisk the flour, baking powder, baking soda and fine sea salt in a medium bowl. Set aside.

Cream the butter and brown sugar in a stand mixer fitted with the paddle attachment. Add the eggs, one at a time. Add the vanilla.

Add the flour mixture to the butter mixture in 3 parts, alternating with the sour cream and ending with the flour mixture. Spread half of this batter in the prepared pan. Sprinkle with half of the topping mixture. Repeat the layers once more.

Bake for about 1 hour or until a wooden skewer comes out of the cake clean.

Cool the cake in the pan for 15 minutes before inverting onto a large serving plate. Cool to room temperature before serving.

Storage: The coffee cake will keep, covered, at room temperature for up to 3 days.

SWEET POTATO AND ZUCCHINI BREAD

Makes 2 loaves

My friend Kristin and I had a fantastic trip to Napa Valley and Sonoma Valley recently. The food and wine were fabulous but the coffee … oh the coffee was divine (for a story about the lengths I will go for coffee, see page 266). On one particular morning we had the most memorable caffè latte and a sweet potato-zucchini loaf that I knew, after one bite, was a must for the book. The bread is moist and slightly dense, laced with cinnamon spice. Perfection!

3 cups (750 mL) all-purpose flour

1 Tbsp (15 mL) ground cinnamon

2 tsp (10 mL) baking soda

1 tsp (5 mL) baking powder

1 tsp (5 mL) ground mace

½ tsp (2.5 mL) fine sea salt

2 cups (500 mL) brown sugar

1 cup (250 mL) vegetable oil

3 eggs

1 Tbsp (15 mL) pure vanilla extract

2 cups (500 mL) grated zucchini

1½ cups (375 mL) cooked and
    mashed sweet potatoes

PREHEAT THE OVEN to 350°F (175°C). Butter and flour two 8- × 4-inch (20 × 10 cm) loaf pans.

Stir together the flour, cinnamon, baking soda, baking powder, mace and salt in a medium bowl. Set aside. In the bowl of a stand mixer fitted with the paddle attachment, add the brown sugar, oil, eggs and vanilla and beat for about 1 minute.

Add the dry ingredients to the egg mixture and beat until combined. Add the zucchini and mashed sweet potatoes and blend until just combined.

Divide the batter evenly into the prepared pans. Bake for about 50 minutes or until a toothpick inserted into the centre of the loaves comes out clean.

Set the pans on a baking rack to cool. Once cool, remove the zucchini bread from the pans. Slice and serve.

Storage: The loaves will keep for 5 days at room temperature if covered in plastic wrap.
To freeze the loaves, cover in plastic wrap and place in a resealable plastic bag.
Store in the freezer for up to 6 months.

VARIATION This recipe can be made into 24 muffins. Bake for about 30 minutes.

JAMMY BREAD PUDDING

Serves 8

This recipe is a good example of what is known as "nursery food": traditional British recipes made for children by their nannies. With all the elements that make comfort food, well, comfortable, this pudding will be appreciated by kids and parents alike.

4 eggs

2 cups (500 mL) half-and-half cream

½ cup (125 mL) milk

2 tsp (10 mL) pure vanilla extract

12 slices good white bread

¼ cup (60 mL) butter, at room temperature

¾–1 cup (185–250 mL) Strawberry-Vanilla or Peach Freezer Jam (pages 234 and 239), or your favourite jam

⅔ cup (160 mL) granulated sugar

PREHEAT THE OVEN to 350°F (175°C). Butter an 8-inch (20 cm) square baking dish and set aside.

Whisk the eggs, cream, milk and vanilla in a medium bowl.

Cut the crusts off of all the slices of bread. Butter one side of each slice of bread. Cut each slice of bread into 4 triangles. Place 1 layer of triangles, butter side down, in the prepared baking dish. Spread a layer of jam on the bread using a knife or the back of a spoon. Pour about one-third of the egg mixture over the first layer of bread. Repeat 2 more layers, finishing the top with a final layer of jam and the remaining egg mixture.

Allow the pudding to sit for at least 15 minutes (overnight is fine). Place the pan into a larger baking dish (I use a 9- × 13-inch [23 × 33 cm] pan for this) and add enough boiling water to come halfway up the pan. Bake the pudding for about 1 hour, or until the pudding is set.

Serve the pudding warm or at room temperature.

Storage: Leftover pudding keeps, covered, in the refrigerator for up to 3 days.

OVERNIGHT PUMPKIN WAFFLES

Makes 6 round waffles

The hardest part of this recipe is remembering to mix up the batter the day before you need it. But if you can jump that hurdle, you're in for a treat. I've started making the batter while I'm preparing dinner. The next morning, the batter has risen nicely and you just add the baking soda.

2 cups (500 mL) all-purpose flour
¼ cup (60 mL) granulated sugar
2 tsp (10 mL) ground cinnamon
1 tsp (5 mL) yeast
½ tsp (2.5 mL) ground mace
  (optional)
½ tsp (2.5 mL) fine sea salt

2 cups (500 mL) buttermilk
1 cup (250 mL) pumpkin purée
2 eggs
¼ cup (60 mL) butter, melted
¼ tsp (1 mL) baking soda
real maple syrup, warmed gently
lightly whipped cream (optional)

COMBINE THE FLOUR, sugar, cinnamon, yeast, mace and salt together in a large bowl. Add the buttermilk, pumpkin purée, eggs and melted butter and mix until well combined. Cover with plastic wrap and refrigerate overnight or at least 8 hours.

In the morning, preheat the waffle iron. Either brush the waffle panels with oil or use a cooking spray.

Whisk the baking soda into the batter and stir until combined. For each waffle, spoon about 1 cup (250 mL) of batter onto the hot waffle iron. Cook the waffle for a few minutes, until it is a crispy golden brown. Remove the waffle from the waffle iron.

Serve with warm maple syrup and, if you are feeling really indulgent, lightly whipped cream.

ROASTED PEAMEAL BACON

Serves 8

When I first met my husband, he introduced me to one of his favourite things: a peameal bacon sandwich from the St. Lawrence Market in Toronto. To this day, whenever he finds himself within a short distance of the market, he will make a special stop. The sandwich is simply thin sliced peameal bacon on a soft Kaiser roll with a squeeze of yellow mustard.

Although this recipe is in the Weekend Brunch chapter, it really could be served at any meal. Roasting a whole piece of peameal bacon is so simple and every slice is juicy with a caramelized peachy-mustard edge. A purist like Alan might not agree, but I think my recipe would make a dreamy peameal bacon sandwich.

2–2½ lb (1–1.25 kg) whole piece
  peameal bacon
½ cup (125 mL) Peach Freezer Jam
  (page 239) or your favourite peach
  or apricot jam

1 Tbsp (15 mL) grainy Dijon mustard
1 tsp (5 mL) finely chopped rosemary

PREHEAT THE OVEN to 400°F (200°C). Line a baking sheet with parchment paper and place a rack on the parchment paper. Place the whole piece of peameal bacon on the rack.

Combine the Peach Freezer Jam, grainy mustard and rosemary in a small bowl. Spread half of the jam mixture on the peameal bacon. Place the peameal bacon in the oven and cook for about 40 minutes. Spread the remaining peach mixture on the meat and return to the oven for another 30 minutes or until a meat thermometer registers 130°F (55°C).

Remove from the oven and let the peameal sit for 10 minutes. Cut into thin slices and serve warm.

TURKEY SAUSAGE PATTIES

Serves 4

Depending on where you live, a good butcher may be hard to come by. I have a very good relationship with my butcher that I have cultivated over several years. Shopping at an independent butcher shop may cost a little more, but I'd rather buy meat from someone I trust and only do business with farmers that adhere to the best farming practices.

To make homemade sausages is to know exactly what you are feeding your family and yourself. They are super easy and you can fiddle with the seasonings to suit your taste. For a Southern-inspired breakfast try a turkey sausage patty on a Cheddar and Red Onion Biscuit (page 27).

FOR THE SAUSAGES

1 lb (500 g) ground turkey

¼ cup (60 mL) chopped chives

1 Tbsp (15 mL) brown sugar

1 tsp (5 mL) fine sea salt

1 tsp (5 mL) fennel seeds, crushed

½ tsp (2.5 mL) smoked paprika

¼ tsp (1 mL) red chili flakes

¼ tsp (1 mL) freshly ground black
    pepper

FOR COOKING

2 Tbsp (30 mL) olive oil

COMBINE ALL OF the sausage ingredients in a large bowl.

Form the mixture into small, thin patties, about 2 inches (5 cm) in diameter. Heat the olive oil in a large cast-iron skillet over medium-high heat. Cook the sausage patties for about 1½ minutes on each side, or until they are cooked through. Serve warm.

VARIATION You don't have to limit yourself to turkey. I've made these sausages with ground chicken and ground pork and both were delicious.

CHEESY POTATO CASSEROLE WITH GRILLED SAUSAGES

Serves 6

This dish is perfect for a cold-weather brunch. Grilled sausages are worth firing up the barbecue for, even in the snow.

3 lb (1.5 kg) Yukon Gold potatoes, peeled and sliced into bite-sized chunks

¼ cup (60 mL) butter

1 cup (250 mL) chopped onion

2 cups (500 mL) chopped mushrooms

¼ cup (60 mL) all-purpose flour

2 cups (500 mL) milk

1½ cups (375 mL) grated sharp cheddar cheese

1 cup (250 mL) sour cream

½ cup (125 mL) chopped green onions

6 large mild Italian or honey garlic sausages

PREHEAT THE OVEN to 375°F (190°C). Butter an 8-inch (20 cm) square baking dish and set aside.

Place the sliced potatoes in a large pot and fill with cold water. Add 1 tsp (5 mL) salt and bring to a boil. Cook the potatoes for about 5 minutes. Drain and set aside.

Melt the butter in a large skillet set over medium heat. Add the onion and cook for about 5 minutes. Add the mushrooms and continue cooking until the mushrooms are soft and cooked through. Lower the heat and sprinkle the onions and mushrooms with the flour; stir to combine. Continue cooking the mixture for a few minutes. Slowly whisk in the milk. Increase the heat to medium and stir the mixture until it has thickened and is smooth. Remove the pan from the heat.

Stir in the cheese, sour cream and green onions. Pour the cheesy mixture over the cooked potatoes and stir to combine. Spoon the potato mixture into the prepared baking dish. Bake for about 35 minutes, or until bubbling.

While the potato casserole is baking, heat the grill. Cook the sausages on the grill until the juices run clear.

Serve the grilled sausages with the hot cheesy potato casserole.

ASPARAGUS AND HAM QUICHE

Serves 8

In 1998, I was put in the enviable position of running a kitchen for the château purchased by the woman I was working for in Vancouver, Linda Meinhardt. Her dream was to turn the château, located in the Limousin Region of France, into a chic Bed & Breakfast and cooking school. Château Drouilles is nestled in the rolling hills of an area known as the "Sheep Capital of France" and it was an experience that I'll never forget.

After cooking at the château, I gained a whole new respect for quiche, as cliché as that may sound. Not only can it be served at any meal, you can change the fillings to match the season. Bon appétit!

1 disc Flaky Pie Dough (page 222)
3 eggs
1½ cups (375 mL) half-and-half
   cream
½ tsp (2.5 mL) fine sea salt
¼ tsp (1 mL) freshly ground black
   pepper

1 cup (250 mL) chopped asparagus,
   lightly blanched for 1 minute in
   boiling water
1 cup (250 mL) chopped ham
1 cup (250 mL) grated Gruyère cheese

PREHEAT THE OVEN to 375°F (190°C).

Roll out the disc of pie dough and fit into a 9-inch (23 cm) deep-dish pie plate, trimming the pastry to ½-inch (1 cm) past the edge of the pie plate. Crimp the edges and set aside.

Whisk the eggs, cream, salt and pepper in a medium bowl.

Fill the pie crust with the blanched asparagus, chopped ham and grated cheese. Pour the egg mixture into the pie crust. Bake for 45 minutes or until the crust is dark golden brown and the filling is set.

Cool the quiche for 5 minutes. Slice and serve warm.

On-The-Go Lunches

Summer Bean Salad   *44*

Quinoa Salad with Roasted Veggies   *45*

Fresh Corn and Cherry Tomato Salad   *47*

Chicken Soup with Rice   *48*

Alphabet Soup   *50*

Lentil and Carrot Soup   *52*

Quick Fried Rice   *53*

Dagwood Sandwiches   *54*

Tomato Hand Tarts   *56*

SUMMER BEAN SALAD

Serves 4

I spent a memorable long weekend in Vancouver doing something a little unusual. I took over the cooking duties for a Bed & Breakfast that was going to be busy with a family wedding. I was there to cook for guests at the B&B, as well as helping to feed the family members that had gathered for the wedding. After that weekend, I have a much greater appreciation of what it takes to run a successful Bed & Breakfast. It may sound relaxing, even a little glamorous, but there is no end to the work that needs to be done.

This salad was, by far, one of the biggest hits of the weekend. It's so simple that I hadn't given it a lot of thought but simple food, done well, is sometimes like that. The key to this salad (and indeed most foods) is getting the amount of salt right. Don't skimp or you aren't going to be happy. And you'll blame the salad . . . or even the author (gasp!).

VINAIGRETTE

1 small clove garlic

1 Tbsp (15 mL) Dijon mustard

1 Tbsp (15 mL) fresh lemon juice

½ tsp (2.5 mL) fine sea salt

¼ tsp (1 mL) freshly ground black pepper

¼ cup (60 mL) extra-virgin olive oil

SALAD

one 14 oz (398 mL) can navy beans or great northern beans, rinsed and drained well

1 cup (250 mL) halved cherry tomatoes

¼ cup (60 mL) finely diced red onion

1 tart apple, cored, peeled and finely chopped

1 ripe avocado, peeled, pitted and sliced

¾ cup (185 mL) crumbled feta cheese

¼ cup (60 mL) chopped fresh basil

MINCE THE GARLIC with a pinch of salt. Whisk the minced garlic, mustard, lemon juice, salt and pepper in a large salad bowl. Slowly add the olive oil to the mixture, whisking constantly. Taste for seasoning.

Place the beans, cherry tomatoes, red onion and chopped apple in the salad bowl with the vinaigrette. Toss together lightly. Gently fold the sliced avocado, feta cheese and fresh basil into the salad. Serve immediately or pack into airtight containers for a delicious lunch.

VARIATION Add 4 cups (1 L) mixed greens (a combination of watercress, baby spinach, mâche or mesclun to the bean salad just before you plan to serve it. Toss well.

QUINOA SALAD WITH ROASTED VEGGIES

Serves 4

Quinoa is known as a "super grain". Its popularity has skyrocketed in recent years, and it's no wonder—quinoa is a complete protein in one little package. People who couldn't pronounce quinoa a few years ago are now eating it by the kilo! Maybe it's the quinoa or maybe it's the roasted vegetables, but I could eat this salad every day of the week.

FOR THE SALAD

4 small zucchini, cut into bite-sized pieces

1 large eggplant, cut into bite-sized pieces

2–3 sweet peppers, cut into bite-sized pieces

⅓ cup (80 mL) olive oil

1½ tsp (7.5 mL) fine sea salt, divided

½ tsp (2.5 mL) freshly ground black pepper

1 cup (250 mL) quinoa

1½ cups (375 mL) water

FOR THE VINAIGRETTE

¼ cup (60 mL) fresh lemon juice

¼ cup (60 mL) extra-virgin olive oil

½ tsp (2.5 mL) fine sea salt

¼ tsp (1 mL) freshly ground black pepper

FOR THE SALAD: Preheat the oven to 400°F (200°C). Line a large baking sheet with parchment paper.

In a medium bowl, toss the chopped vegetables with the olive oil, 1 tsp (5 mL) salt and pepper. Spread the veggies on the prepared baking sheet and roast for about 35 minutes or until the veggies are cooked through and start to caramelize. Let cool.

Rinse the quinoa in a sieve under cold water. Bring the water to a boil in a medium saucepan. Add the quinoa and remaining ½ tsp (2.5 mL) salt and return to a boil. Reduce the heat to low, cover the pot and continue cooking for 15 minutes. Turn the heat off and leave the quinoa in the covered pot for another 5 minutes.

Line a baking sheet with paper towels and spread the quinoa out to cool and dry.

FOR THE VINAIGRETTE: Whisk the lemon juice, olive oil, salt and pepper together in a medium bowl.

To serve the salad, toss the quinoa, roasted veggies and vinaigrette together and serve cold or at room temperature.

Storage: This salad can be made the day before you plan to serve it.

FRESH CORN AND CHERRY TOMATO SALAD

Serves 4

Bright red cherry tomatoes mingling with fresh yellow corn kernels in a Mexican-inspired vinaigrette make for a salad that is as tasty as it is beautiful. We are lucky to have several farms nearby that grow and sell sweet corn, spoiling us against anything that remotely looks like it's been imported. I recommend making this salad at the height of sweet corn season—August and September.

FOR THE SALAD

6 cobs of fresh sweet corn

1 cup (250 mL) halved cherry tomatoes

1/2 cup (125 mL) finely chopped green onions

1/2 cup (125 mL) chopped cilantro

1 cup (250 mL) crumbled Macedonian feta cheese

FOR THE VINAIGRETTE

3 Tbsp (45 mL) fresh lime juice

3 Tbsp (45 mL) extra-virgin olive oil

1/2 tsp (2.5 mL) chili powder

1/2 tsp (2.5 mL) fine sea salt

1/4 tsp (1 mL) freshly ground black pepper

FOR THE SALAD: Bring a stockpot of water to a boil. Blanch the corncobs in the boiling water for 5 minutes. Remove from the pot and let cool.

Cut the kernels off the cobs and place in a large bowl. Add the cherry tomatoes, green onions, cilantro and feta cheese.

FOR THE VINAIGRETTE: Whisk the lime juice, olive oil, chili powder, salt and pepper together in a small bowl. Pour the vinaigrette over the salad and toss gently. Serve immediately.

CHICKEN SOUP WITH RICE

Serves 6

There is a little book of poems called Chicken Soup with Rice: A Book of Months by Maurice Sendak that my sister and I read over and over again when we were kids. My mom ordered it for us from the Scholastic Book flyers that are still handed out in classrooms today. It was probably the best few dollars she ever spent on a book and we still love reading it with our kids today. It was that little book that inspired this recipe.

2 Tbsp (30 mL) olive oil

1½ cups (375 mL) finely chopped onion

1 cup (250 mL) finely chopped celery

10 cups (2.5 L) Chicken Stock (page 251)

1½ cups (375 mL) carrots, cut into coins

1 bay leaf

2 tsp (10 mL) fine sea salt

1 lb (500 g) cooked boneless, skinless chicken breast, cut into bite-sized pieces (see sidebar)

¾ cup (185 mL) uncooked basmati rice

1 Tbsp (15 mL) soy sauce

fine sea salt

HEAT THE OIL in a large stockpot over medium heat. Add the onion and celery and cook until soft. Add the chicken stock, carrots, bay leaf and salt and bring to a boil. Reduce the heat and simmer for about 30 minutes, uncovered.

Add the chicken, rice and soy sauce and simmer for about 20 minutes longer, covered. Taste the soup and add more salt if necessary. Remove the bay leaf. Serve hot.

Storage: Store leftover soup, covered, in the refrigerator for up to 5 days, or freeze leftover soup in airtight containers for up to 6 months.

To cook the boneless, skinless chicken breast, preheat the oven to 375°F (190°C). Season the chicken with salt and pepper and place on a baking sheet. Cover with tin foil and bake for about 30 minutes. Allow the chicken to cool and cut the chicken into bite-sized pieces.

If you have made your chicken stock with a Basted Beer-Can Chicken (page xx) or a roasted chicken, you can omit the soy sauce in this recipe.

In January / It's so nice
While slipping / On the sliding ice
To sip hot chicken soup with rice.

Sipping once / Sipping twice
Sipping chicken soup / With rice.

— FROM *Chicken Soup with Rice: A Book of Months* BY MAURICE SENDAK

ALPHABET SOUP

Makes 6 servings

There is something so fun about seeing (and eating) little letters of the alphabet in this tomato-based soup. My kids like to hunt for their initials and it's always a big hit when they show their friends at school.

1 Tbsp (15 mL) olive oil
1 cup (250 mL) finely diced onion
½ cup (125 mL) finely diced carrot
½ cup (125 mL) finely diced celery
2 cloves garlic, minced
1 tsp (5 mL) fine sea salt
¼ tsp (1 mL) freshly ground black pepper

5 cups (1.25 L) Chicken or Veggie Stock (pages 251 and 252)
1 cup (250 mL) bottled strained tomatoes (passata) or tomato juice
½ cup (125 mL) uncooked alphabet pasta
1 Tbsp (15 mL) Worcestershire sauce

HEAT THE OLIVE oil in a large saucepan over medium heat. Add the onion, carrot and celery and cook for about 5 minutes until the vegetables are softened. Add the garlic and salt and continue cooking for a few more minutes.

Add the stock and passata and bring to a boil. Reduce the heat and simmer the soup for about 10 minutes. Add the alphabet pasta. Simmer for another 5 minutes. Add the Worcestershire sauce and season with salt and pepper. Serve hot.

LENTIL AND CARROT SOUP

Serves 6

One November I made a weekend trip to see my friends, Elaine and Dermot, in Newfoundland. My plane was diverted to an out-of-the-way airport, about 2 hours from their house. Instead of staying on the plane and letting the airline dictate my fate, I walked off the plane, leaving my luggage behind (it was a liberating moment!). I grabbed a ride with some people who were going to be driving right past my destination and when I arrived Elaine was waiting at the door, a glass of champagne in her hand. She served a lentil soup during the weekend that really hit the spot and this recipe reminds me of that soup and their wonderful Newfoundland hospitality. I would happily desert my luggage for another Newfoundland weekend and a bowl of lentil and carrot soup.

¼ cup (60 mL) butter

2 Tbsp (30 mL) olive oil

4 cups (1 L) chopped onions

2 cups (500 mL) chopped carrots

1 cup (250 mL) chopped celery

1 Tbsp (15 mL) minced garlic

1 Tbsp (15 mL) ground cumin

2 tsp (10 mL) fine sea salt

½ tsp (2.5 mL) freshly ground
  black pepper

2 cups (500 mL) brown or yellow
  lentils

8 cups (2 L) Chicken or Veggie Stock
  (pages 251 and 252) (approx)

juice of 1 lemon

HEAT A LARGE stockpot over medium heat. Add the butter and olive oil. Cook the onions in the stockpot over medium-low heat for about 30 minutes or until the onions start to turn golden and caramelized.

Add the carrots, celery, garlic, cumin, salt and pepper and cook for about 5 minutes, stirring occasionally, or until the veggies are soft.

Add the lentils and chicken stock and bring to a boil. Simmer over low heat for about 40 minutes, adding up to 4 cups (1 L) of more chicken stock or water if the soup is getting too thick. When the lentils are cooked through, add the lemon juice and taste for seasoning, adding more salt if necessary.

QUICK FRIED RICE

Serves 4

Quick fried rice has been my busy-night dinner for years. One morning I was struggling with what to send in the kids' lunches and I had an epiphany—make quick fried rice and pack it into insulated containers. They loved it! When the weather is cold, this dish hits all the right notes—hot, healthy, quick—and it's a great way to use up leftovers.

3 Tbsp (45 mL) grape seed oil

6 cups (1.5 L) cooked Basmati Rice (see below)

1/3 cup (80 mL) good soy sauce or tamari

2 eggs

2/3 cup (160 mL) chopped green onions

HEAT THE OIL in a large cast-iron skillet over medium-high heat. Add the rice and reduce the heat to medium. Stir the rice, using a spatula to scrape any bits off the pan. Add the soy sauce and mix into the rice. Crack the eggs on top of the rice mixture and mix it all up. By now the rice mixture should be nice and hot. Add the chopped green onions and stir to combine. Serve immediately or pack into thermoses for later.

> VARIATION Feel free to add more ingredients to the rice, such as chopped ham, cooked veggies, finely chopped mushrooms or cubed tofu.
>
> FOR PERFECT BASMATI RICE, rinse 1½ cups (375 mL) basmati rice under cool water. Place the rice in a medium saucepan with 2¼ cups (560 mL) warm water and let sit for 20 minutes. Bring the rice and water to a boil, add 1 tsp (5 mL) butter and reduce heat to low. Cover and cook for 8 minutes. Remove from the heat and let stand for a few minutes. Fluff the rice gently with a fork and serve or cool and store in an airtight container in the refrigerator for up to 3 days. Makes 6 cups.

DAGWOOD SANDWICHES

Serves 4

I remember reading the Blondie *comic strips in the newspaper when I was a kid. There was a character in the comic named Dagwood Bumstead (what a great name!) and he was often shown eating HUGE sandwiches full of cold cuts, cheeses and veggies. A true to life Dagwood sandwich would be impossible to get your mouth around but this version will be perfect for all members of your family.*

1 fresh baguette
Homemade Mayonnaise (page 250),
   as desired
grainy mustard, as desired
½ lb (250 g) Black Forest ham, thinly
   sliced
½ lb (250 g) mortadella
¼ lb (125 g) German salami, thinly
   sliced

½ lb (250 g) sharp cheddar
   cheese, sliced
12 thin slices ripe tomatoes, or
   enough to fill the sandwich
½ cup (125 mL) thinly sliced red
   onion, or to taste
¼ cup (60 mL) thinly sliced green
   olives with pimentos

SLICE THE BAGUETTE lengthwise horizontally, leaving a little bit of the baguette attached on one side. Spread the mayonnaise and the grainy mustard over the insides of the baguette to taste.

Layer the ham, mortadella, salami, cheese, tomatoes, red onion and green olives on the baguette. Close the sandwich as well as you can and cut into four 6-inch (15 cm) pieces. Serve immediately, or wrap in parchment paper or plastic wrap and pack into lunch bags and refrigerate until needed.

TOMATO HAND TARTS

Makes 6 individual tarts

These tarts are for times when you want something a little more special than just sand-wiches. I took a couple batches of these to an afternoon at the go-kart track and everyone felt very spoiled. Caramelized onions, olives, goat cheese—picnic baskets have never had it so good. Better make more of these than you think you're going to need.

3 Tbsp (45 mL) olive oil

2 cups (500 mL) thinly sliced red
onions

1 tsp (5 mL) fresh thyme leaves

1 roll butter puff pastry

1 egg, beaten

¼ cup (60 mL) finely diced Kalamata
olives

12 slices fresh goat cheese, or
enough for 6 tarts

18 cherry tomatoes, halved

fine sea salt

freshly ground black pepper

2 Tbsp (30 mL) finely chopped
fresh chives

HEAT THE OLIVE oil in a large cast-iron skillet over medium heat. Caramelize the onions until golden brown; this will take about 30 minutes. Add the thyme about 5 minutes before the onions are finished. Set aside.

Preheat the oven to 425°F (220°C). Unroll the puff pastry sheet and cut into 6 equal portions. Place on a baking sheet. Using a sharp knife, score an inner line on each of the portions about 1 cm from the edge. Brush the pastry with the beaten egg. Bake for 8 minutes or until golden brown.

Spoon the caramelized onions into the centre of each tartlet. If the puff pastry has puffed, placing the onions in the centre will flatten the tartlet, leaving a puffy crust. Sprinkle the olives on the onions. Place the goat cheese slices over the onions and olives. Place 6 cherry tomato halves on top of each tart. Sprinkle with salt and pepper.

Return the tarts to the oven and bake for another 10 minutes until the cheese begins to melt. Remove from the oven and sprinkle with the chopped chives. Serve warm or at room temperature.

Staying-Put Lunches

Grilled Chicken and Double Smoked Bacon Salad   *61*

Romaine Salad with Creamy Italian Dressing
   and Fresh Garlic Croutons   *62*

Green Pea Salad with Mint and Goat Cheese   *64*

Kale Tabbouleh   *67*

Curried Coconut Chicken Soup   *68*

Broccoli-Cheddar Soup   *70*

Hand-Pressed Chicken Burger Patties   *71*

Grilled Pimento-Cheese Sandwiches   *72*

Tuna Melts   *74*

Baked Mac and Cheese   *75*

GRILLED CHICKEN AND DOUBLE SMOKED BACON SALAD

Serves 6

This salad will satisfy the hungriest of people. While you are grilling the chicken, why not make some Grilled Bread (page 100) to serve with the salad. Oh, and a Rhubarb Gin and Tonic (page 260) would be a lovely way to start a weekend lunch.

FOR THE SALAD

2 boneless, skinless chicken breasts

fine sea salt

freshly ground black pepper

6 slices double-smoked bacon, or
   your favourite bacon

8 cups (2 L) salad greens (a
   combination of green and red leaf,
   romaine or bibb lettuce)

1 bunch watercress

3 tomatoes, cut into wedges

1 ripe avocado, sliced

½ cup (125 mL) finely chopped green
   onions

1 cup (250 mL) diced feta cheese

FOR THE VINAIGRETTE

⅓ cup (80 mL) freshly squeezed
   lemon juice

1 Tbsp (15 mL) Dijon mustard

1 clove garlic, minced

½ cup (125 mL) extra-virgin olive oil

½ tsp (2.5 mL) fine sea salt

¼ tsp (1 mL) freshly ground black
   pepper

FOR THE SALAD: Heat the grill. Generously sprinkle the chicken breasts with salt and pepper. Slowly cook the chicken over indirect heat to avoid burning. When the chicken is cooked through, remove from the grill and let cool for 10 minutes. Slice the chicken into thin strips.

Cook the bacon in a cast-iron skillet over medium-high heat until crisp. Chop the bacon into bite-sized pieces. Place the greens and the watercress on a large platter. Arrange the chicken, bacon, tomatoes, avocado and green onions on the salad. Top with feta cheese.

FOR THE VINAIGRETTE: Whisk the lemon juice, mustard and garlic together in a small bowl. Slowly pour the olive oil into the lemon juice mixture and whisk until incorporated. Add the salt and pepper. Check for seasoning and add more salt if necessary.

Just before serving, drizzle the vinaigrette over the salad and gently toss.

Serve immediately.

A 375°F (190°C) oven cooks bacon evenly and without all the greasy spatters.

ROMAINE SALAD WITH CREAMY ITALIAN DRESSING AND FRESH GARLIC CROUTONS

Serves 6

Here is another option for making homemade salad dressing. Salad dressings (and vinaigrettes) are so easy to make but it's easy to forget to plan ahead. If you can make your salad dressing ahead of time, you won't find yourself reaching for store-bought options all the time. And just so you don't start to hate me, you should know that I do keep a couple bottles on hand, just in case!

I better mention that the garlic croutons are extremely addictive and I've been known to make a meal of them before dinner. Not a good move.

10 cups (2.5 L) romaine salad leaves, or a combination of other sturdy leafy greens, chopped

1½ cups (375 mL) halved cherry tomatoes

1 English cucumber, quartered lengthwise and chopped into bite-sized pieces

½ cup (125 mL) Creamy Italian Dressing (recipe follows) (approx)

2 cups (500 mL) Fresh Garlic Croutons (recipe follows)

PLACE THE CHOPPED romaine lettuce into a large salad-serving bowl. Top with the cherry tomatoes and cucumber pieces. Drizzle the Creamy Italian Dressing over the salad and toss to lightly coat the salad greens. Add more dressing if needed. Add the croutons and gently toss to combine. Serve immediately.

CREAMY ITALIAN DRESSING

Makes about 1 cup (250 mL)

1/3 cup (80 mL) Homemade Mayonnaise (page 250)
1/3 cup (80 mL) plain whole-milk yogurt
2 Tbsp (30 mL) minced red onion
2 Tbsp (30 mL) minced parsley
1 Tbsp (15 mL) balsamic vinegar
1 Tbsp (15 mL) red wine vinegar
3/4 tsp (4 mL) dried oregano
1/2 tsp (2.5 mL) fine sea salt
1/4 tsp (1 mL) freshly ground black pepper

COMBINE ALL OF the ingredients in the bowl of a food processor and process until smooth. Use immediately or store in an airtight container for up to 3 days.

Storage: Keep covered in the refrigerator for up to 4 days.

FRESH GARLIC CROUTONS

Makes about 2 cups (500 mL)

2 Tbsp (30 mL) butter
2 Tbsp (30 mL) extra-virgin olive oil
2 cloves garlic, minced
1/4 tsp (1 mL) fine sea salt
2 cups (500 mL) bite-sized pieces of day-old crusty bread

HEAT THE BUTTER and olive oil in a large cast-iron skillet over medium-low heat. Add the minced garlic and cook for a few minutes, until the garlic starts to soften but doesn't colour. Add the bread pieces and toss in the pan, cooking for several minutes until the bread starts to get crunchy and golden. Sprinkle with salt. Remove from the pan and spread on a baking sheet to cool.

Storage: These croutons are best eaten the day they are made.

GREEN PEA SALAD WITH MINT AND GOAT CHEESE

Serves 6

The original recipe for this salad was given to me by my Aunt Ellen, who got it from my grandma. I love the way good recipes make their way from generation to generation. It had been off my radar for several years when I decided to serve it at a dinner party we were having. One friend practically licked the bowl clean and insisted on getting the recipe before she left that night.

Frozen peas are a major time saver in the kitchen. If you do have fresh peas from the garden, enlist anyone who claims to be bitten by the "summer boredom bug" for shelling!

4 cups (1 L) fresh or frozen green peas

½ cup (125 mL) finely chopped green onions

½ cup (125 mL) finely chopped celery

¼ cup (60 mL) grape seed oil

¼ cup (60 mL) white wine vinegar

½ tsp (2.5 mL) granulated sugar

½ tsp (2.5 mL) fine sea salt

⅛ tsp (0.5 mL) freshly ground black pepper

3 Tbsp (45 mL) chopped fresh mint

½ cup (125 mL) crumbled goat cheese

COVER THE FROZEN peas with boiling water and let stand 2 minutes. Drain well. Place the peas in a large bowl and add the green onions and celery.

In a separate bowl, combine the oil, vinegar, sugar, salt and pepper. Pour the mixture over the vegetables and toss well. At this point the salad can be refrigerated for 1–2 hours or it can be served immediately. Just before serving, add the chopped mint and goat cheese and toss gently.

KALE TABBOULEH

Serves 6

A traditional tabbouleh is a chopped parsley salad combined with bulgur wheat, tomatoes and cucumbers. Kale is such a hardy green that when you grind it in the food processor the results look exactly like chopped parsley. Not only is kale incredibly good for you, the food processor saves a ton of chopping time. Substituting kale for parsley was a light-bulb moment for me, and this salad was the result.

FOR THE SALAD

1 cup (250 mL) bulgur

½ tsp (2.5 mL) fine sea salt

1¼ cups (310 mL) boiling water

1 bunch fresh kale

1 cup (250 mL) finely diced tomatoes

½ cup (125 mL) finely sliced green
 onions

½ cup (125 mL) crumbled feta cheese

FOR THE VINAIGRETTE

¼ cup (60 mL) fresh lemon juice

¼ cup (60 mL) extra-virgin olive oil

½ tsp (2.5 mL) fine sea salt

¼ tsp (1 mL) freshly ground black
 pepper

FOR THE SALAD: Combine the bulgur and salt in a medium bowl. Pour the boiling water over the bulgur, cover with plastic wrap and let sit for about 20 minutes or until all of the water has been absorbed.

Cut the hard rib from each piece of kale and discard the rib. Tear the kale leaves into smaller pieces. Place about a third of the kale into the work bowl of a food processor and process until it is finely chopped. The kale should look like chopped parsley. Scrape the finely chopped kale into a large bowl and continue chopping the kale in batches.

Layer the chopped kale, cooked bulgur, diced tomatoes, green onions and feta cheese on a large serving plate.

FOR THE VINAIGRETTE: Whisk the lemon juice, olive oil, salt and pepper in a medium bowl. Pour the vinaigrette over the salad and toss thoroughly.

CURRIED COCONUT CHICKEN SOUP

Serves 8

Also known as mulligatawny soup, this dish was made famous during the British Raj in India. I served two versions of mulligatawny at a Celtic dinner class I was teaching and this was the hands down favourite. It's a soup that will warm you from head to toe.

3 Tbsp (45 mL) butter

1 cup (250 mL) finely chopped onions

1 cup (250 mL) finely chopped carrot

1½ cups (375 mL) peeled and chopped tart apples (such as Granny Smith)

3 Tbsp (45 mL) all-purpose flour

2 tsp (10 mL) curry powder

8 cloves

10 cups (2.5 L) Chicken Stock (page 251)

1½ tsp (7.5 mL) fine sea salt

one 28 oz (796 mL) can diced tomatoes, drained

2 cups (500 mL) cooked, bite-sized pieces chicken (see page 48)

⅓ cup (80 mL) dried currants

⅓ cup (80 mL) uncooked basmati rice

1 cup (250 mL) coconut milk

MELT THE BUTTER in a large stockpot over medium heat. Add the onions and carrots and cook for a few minutes until soft. Add the chopped apple and continue cooking for 5 minutes.

Stir in the flour, curry powder and cloves. Cook for about 2 minutes, stirring often. Add the chicken stock and salt and bring to a boil. Reduce the heat and simmer for 20 minutes, stirring occasionally.

Add the diced tomatoes, cooked chicken and currants and continue cooking for another 10 minutes or so. Add the rice and coconut milk. Stir and simmer for another 15 minutes. Taste the soup for seasoning and remove the cloves. Serve hot.

BROCCOLI-CHEDDAR SOUP

Makes 12 cups (3 L)

I like the combination of broccoli and cheddar cheese so much, I gave it its own recipe in the Sides chapter (page 109). This soup is made in two parts. The first is the broccoli purée and the second is the cheese sauce. When the two come together, well, it's hardly surprising that this is my family's favourite soup.

¼ cup + 2 Tbsp (60 mL + 30 mL) butter

2 cups (500 mL) chopped onions

1½ cups (375 mL) chopped celery

8 cups (2 L) chopped broccoli stems and crowns (remove any woody parts of the stalk)

6 cups (1.5 L) Chicken Stock (page 251)

2 Tbsp (30 mL) all-purpose flour

3 cups (750 mL) whole milk

1 cup (250 mL) whipping cream

3 cups (750 mL) grated sharp cheddar cheese

MELT ¼ CUP (60 mL) butter in a large stockpot over medium heat. Add the onions and celery and cook for about 10 minutes, until very soft. Add the broccoli and cook for another few minutes. Add the chicken stock and bring to a boil. Simmer for about 15 minutes, until the broccoli is soft.

Meanwhile, melt the remaining 2 Tbsp (30 mL) butter in a medium saucepan. Add the flour and cook over medium-low heat for about 3 minutes. Slowly add the milk, whisking constantly. Cook the sauce over medium heat until it is bubbling and thick. Remove from the heat. Add the cream and grated cheese and stir to combine. Set aside.

Purée the broccoli mixture using an immersion blender or in batches in a food processor. Combine the puréed broccoli mixture with the cheese sauce in the large stockpot. Serve hot but do not bring to a boil.

VARIATION For a vegetarian version, I've made this soup with water instead of chicken stock. Remember to check your seasoning.

If you want to freeze this soup, do so before adding the cheese mixture.

HAND-PRESSED CHICKEN BURGER PATTIES

Makes 8 burger patties

I went to high school with Jamie Waldron, co-author of The Home Butchering Handbook *(Penguin, 2013). I heard through the grapevine that Jamie makes really good chicken burgers so I was thrilled when he agreed to give me this recipe.*

2 lb (1 kg) ground chicken	2 Tbsp (30 mL) Dijon mustard
1 cup (250 mL) Fresh Bread Crumbs (see below)	1 Tbsp (15 mL) honey
¾ cup (185 mL) finely chopped green onions	1 tsp (5 mL) fine sea salt
	½ tsp (2.5 mL) freshly ground black pepper

HEAT THE GRILL to about 400°F (200°C).

Gently combine all of the ingredients together. Shape the burger mixture into eight ½-inch (1 cm) thick patties. Each patty will be about 4 oz (120 g).

Grill the chicken patties for about 5 minutes on each side, or until the juices run clear.

Serve the chicken burgers on fresh buns with sliced tomato, green lettuce and Homemade Mayonnaise (page 250).

Storage: If you are making the chicken burgers ahead of time, place each patty on a square piece of parchment paper. Stack the patties and wrap the stack well. Freeze for up to 3 months.

VARIATION To make great chicken nuggets divide the mixture into 1 oz (30 g) portions and flatten to create nuggets. Coat in bread crumbs and pan-fry in a cast-iron skillet.

BREAD CRUMBS are one of those ingredients that you don't think about until you actually need them. Considering most of us have bread kicking around that we aren't going to use before it goes stale, making bread crumbs should be something that becomes second nature.

FRESH BREAD CRUMBS are made from fresh or day-old bread that hasn't been dried out. If the crust is crispy or hard, you may want to cut the crusts off. Place slices of soft bread in the food processor. Process until the crumbs can't get any smaller. Freeze in a sealed container for up to 3 months.

DRY BREAD CRUMBS are made from bread that has been dried out to a crisp. Place the bread on a large baking sheet and bake in a 300°F (150°C) oven for up to 30 minutes, checking periodically to avoid burning the bread. Remove the bread from the oven and let cool. Place the toasted bread in the food processor and process until the crumbs are very small, almost like sand. Store in a sealed container for up to 1 month.

. . . .

GRILLED PIMENTO-CHEESE SANDWICHES

Makes 4 sandwiches

Why should the southern United States have pimento cheese all to themselves? The combination of sharp cheddar cheese and pimentos (or roasted red peppers) is startlingly delicious, and versatile too. Serve pimento cheese on veggies, crackers, sandwiches, burgers or in these grilled cheese sandwiches. I've even served ham and pimento cheese sandwiches at a fancy afternoon tea to rave reviews.

FOR THE PIMENTO CHEESE

⅔ cup (160 mL) pimentos

½ cup (125 mL) Homemade
   Mayonnaise (page 250)

1 Tbsp (15 mL) finely minced onions

1 tsp (5 mL) Worcestershire sauce

¼ tsp (1 mL) freshly ground black
   pepper

12 oz (375 g) sharp extra old cheddar
   cheese, grated

FOR THE SANDWICHES

½ cup (125 mL) butter, at room
   temperature

8 slices rustic bread

2 Granny Smith apples, peeled, cored
   and thinly sliced

PLACE THE PIMENTOS, mayonnaise, onions, Worcestershire sauce and pepper in the work bowl of a food processor. Process the mixture until smooth. Add the grated cheese and process again until combined well. Cover and refrigerate the pimento cheese for at least an hour.

Heat a cast-iron skillet over medium heat. Butter 1 side of each slice of bread. Spread 3–4 Tbsp (45–60 mL) of pimento cheese on the opposite side of 2 of the buttered slices. Place these bread slices, butter side down, in the heated pan. Top with a few slices of apple and the other pieces of buttered bread, butter side up. Cook the sandwich until the bread is toasted and crispy. Flip the sandwich and continue cooking until the sandwich is evenly cooked.

Allow the sandwich to sit for a few minutes before cutting into triangles. Serve with Pickled Green Beans (page 249).

Storage: Cover any remaining pimento cheese and refrigerate for up to 1 week.

PIMENTO-CHEESE WELSH RAREBIT Spread ⅓ cup (80 mL) pimento cheese on a thick sliced piece of bread. Broil for 2–3 minutes and serve hot.

Pimentos are a variety of sweet red chili peppers, arguably best known for being stuffed into green olives. Roasted red peppers are a good substitute.

· · · · · · · · · · ·

TUNA MELTS

Serves 6

I remember Fridays being the day that my dad would meet us at our grandparent's house for lunch. Grandma McDonald was such a good cook, almost anything was appreciated, but I particularly loved her tuna melts. The cheesy-tuna mixture was scooped onto super fresh English muffins and popped into the toaster oven for heating through. What an incredibly satisfying lunch they made. Over the years I've tweaked the recipe and I think Grandma would have approved.

two 6 oz (175 g) cans tuna, drained and flaked

1½ cups (375 mL) finely shredded Swiss cheese, divided

½ cup (125 mL) Homemade Mayonnaise (page 250)

½ cup (125 mL) finely chopped green onions

¼ cup (60 mL) finely chopped dill pickle

1 Tbsp (15 mL) fresh lemon juice

½ tsp (2.5 mL) Worcestershire sauce

2–3 dashes hot sauce

6 English muffins, split and lightly toasted

paprika, for dusting

IN A MEDIUM bowl, mix together the tuna, 1 cup (250 mL) Swiss cheese, mayonnaise, green onions, dill pickle, lemon juice, Worcestershire sauce and hot sauce. Spread about ¼ cup (60 mL) of the filling on each piece of lightly toasted English muffin. Sprinkle each piece with the remaining cheese and a dash of paprika. Broil about 3 inches (8 cm) from source of heat for 2–3 minutes or until cheese is melted and bubbly. Serve hot.

We don't always need this many tuna melts for 1 meal so I save the leftover filling and spread it on crackers for a snack.

BAKED MAC AND CHEESE

Serves 6

This is my go-to dish when we have friends over for lunch and quite often there is an epiphany that happens. Who knew that homemade mac and cheese could be this scrumptious? The secret is in using the most flavourful aged cheddar you can find. There are very few dishes as comforting and nostalgic as this one.

1 lb (500 g) macaroni noodles
splash extra-virgin olive oil
4 cups (1 L) milk
½ cup + 2 Tbsp (125 mL + 30 mL) unsalted butter
½ cup (125 mL) all-purpose flour

6 cups (1.5 L) grated aged cheddar cheese
1 Tbsp (15 mL) fine sea salt
1 tsp (5 mL) freshly ground black pepper
1 cup (250 mL) Fresh Bread Crumbs (page 71)

PREHEAT THE OVEN to 375°F (190°C).

Cook the noodles in a big pot of salted water until tender but still a little chewy. Drain and toss with olive oil. Set aside.

Warm the milk over medium heat. Do not boil.

Melt ½ cup (125 mL) butter in a large pot. Stir in the flour using a wooden spoon and cook for 2 minutes, continuing to stir. Whisk in the warm milk and continue whisking until the sauce is thickened and smooth. Remove from the heat and add the cheddar cheese, salt and pepper.

Add the cooked pasta, stir well and pour into a 9- × 13-inch (23 × 33 cm) baking dish.

Melt remaining 2 Tbsp (30 mL) butter in a small saucepan. Stir the bread crumbs into the melted butter and sprinkle on top of the macaroni and cheese.

Bake in the oven for 30 minutes or until the bread crumbs are golden brown and the sauce is bubbling.

Let stand at room temperature for 5 minutes before serving. Serve hot.

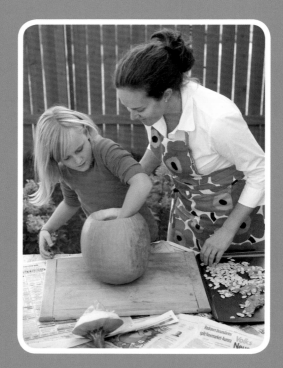

Snacks
and Treats

Roasted Pumpkin Seeds   *78*

Home-Popped Kettle Corn   *80*

Ranger Cookies   *81*

Lavender Shortbread Jam Sandwiches   *83*

Animal Crackers   *84*

Strawberry Ice Pops   *86*

Chocolate Pudding   *87*

Vanilla Bean Tapioca Pudding   *88*

Pretzel Caramels   *89*

Peanut Butter Chocolate Squares   *91*

ROASTED PUMPKIN SEEDS

Makes 2 cups (500 mL)

One the most popular autumn activities for families is heading out to the pumpkin patch and picking out the perfect specimens for Hallowe'en jack-o-lanterns. My pumpkin patch policy is to allow the kids to pick out whichever pumpkin they want, as long as they can get it back to the car by themselves. It's fun to see everyone debating over their choices. When it's time for carving the pumpkins, scoop out the seeds and save them for this addictive little snack.

2 cups (500 mL) fresh pumpkin seeds, scooped out of a fresh pumpkin (approx)

2 Tbsp + ½ tsp (30 mL + 2 mL) fine sea salt

2 Tbsp (30 mL) coconut oil, melted

PREHEAT THE OVEN to 375°F (190°C). Place the pumpkin seeds in a small saucepan and cover with cold water. Add 2 Tbsp (30 mL) salt and bring to a boil. Lower the heat and simmer for 10 minutes.

Strain the seeds and spread them out on a baking sheet covered with paper towels. Blot the pumpkin seeds with another piece of paper towel until the seeds are dry.

Place the dry pumpkin seeds on a baking sheet lined with parchment paper. Drizzle with the melted coconut oil and roast in the oven for about 10 minutes. Stir the seeds around and continue roasting for another 10 minutes or so, until they are crisp and light golden brown. If you hear the pumpkin seeds popping in the oven, it's time for them to come out.

Sprinkle the hot pumpkin seeds with the remaining ½ tsp (2.5 mL) salt and toss to coat. Cool the pumpkin seeds to room temperature.

Storage: The pumpkin seeds will keep in an airtight container for up to 3 weeks.

HOME-POPPED KETTLE CORN

Makes about 24 cups (6 L)

My husband, Alan, once bought a 50-pound bag of popcorn kernels from a local farm. It made great popcorn but it was about 48 pounds more than we needed. We were giving away bags of kernels for months but our friends weren't complaining!

⅓ cup (80 mL) grape seed oil	2 Tbsp (30 mL) granulated sugar
1 cup (250 mL) yellow popcorn kernels	¼ cup (60 mL) melted butter
	¼ tsp (1 mL) fine sea salt, or to taste

PLACE THE OIL in a large stockpot over high heat (the stockpot needs a lid but don't place it on the pot yet). Add 1 popcorn kernel. When the kernel pops, the oil is ready. Add the remaining popcorn and sprinkle with sugar. Reduce the heat to medium-high.

Cover the pot with the lid slightly ajar and place back over the heat. Carefully shake the pot a few times until the kernels start to pop. Continue shaking continuously until the popping slows down, about 3 minutes.

Dump the popcorn into a large bowl. Drizzle with the melted butter and sprinkle with fine sea salt. Serve warm.

RANGER COOKIES

Makes 2 dozen cookies

RANGER COOKIE *(noun): a thin, chewy cookie, crispy around the edges; chock full of rice crisps, coconut and oats; been around for years; enjoying a bit of a comeback lately.*

½ cup (125 mL) all-purpose flour

1 tsp (5 mL) baking powder

½ tsp (2.5 mL) fine sea salt

½ cup (125 mL) butter, at room temperature

½ cup (125 mL) brown sugar

½ cup (125 mL) granulated sugar

1 egg

1 tsp (5 mL) pure vanilla extract

1 cup (250 mL) puffed rice cereal

1 cup (250 mL) rolled oats

½ cup (125 mL) shredded coconut

PREHEAT THE OVEN to 350°F (175°C). Line 2 baking sheets with parchment paper and set aside.

Combine the flour, baking powder and salt and set aside.

Cream the butter and sugars together in the work bowl of a stand mixer fitted with the paddle attachment. Add the egg and vanilla and mix until incorporated. Add the flour mixture and continue to mix. Add the puffed rice, rolled oats and coconut and mix until combined.

Scoop 2 Tbsp (30 mL) of cookie dough per cookie onto the baking sheets. Press down gently. Bake for 10–12 minutes. The cookies are ready when they are golden around the edges.

Storage: Store the cookies in an airtight container for up to 1 week.

LAVENDER SHORTBREAD JAM SANDWICHES

Makes 3 dozen sandwiches

Lavender is one of my absolute favourite herbs in anything, but especially baking. These are the sweetest little cookies. My sister suggested that I sell these cookies but I can't keep them around long enough. They make excellent gifts, though.

2¼ cups (560 mL) all-purpose flour

1 Tbsp (15 mL) dried lavender flowers

1 cup (250 mL) butter, at room temperature

¾ cup (185 mL) granulated sugar

½ tsp (2.5 mL) fine sea salt

½ cup (125 mL) Two-Burner Raspberry Jam (page 243) or another red berry jam (approx)

PREHEAT THE OVEN to 300°F (150°C). Line a large baking sheet with parchment paper.

Whisk the flour and dried lavender flowers together in a small bowl.

Cream the butter, sugar and salt in the bowl of a stand mixer fitted with the paddle attachment. Slowly add the dry ingredients to the butter mixture. Beat the dough on medium speed until it begins to come together in a ball.

Scrape the dough out onto a lightly floured surface. Divide the dough in half, using half for the bottoms of the sandwiches and half for the tops.

Roll one-half of the dough out to a thickness of about ⅛–¼-inch (3–6 mm). Using a Linzer cookie cutter, cut out as many bottoms as you can get. Press the scraps together and gently reroll, trying not to use too much extra flour. Repeat the process with the second half, cutting out tops with decorative shapes in the centre (see sidebar).

Bake for 15–18 minutes, or until the cookies start to turn golden around the edges. Remove from the oven and let cool to room temperature.

Spread a thin layer of jam on the bottom cookies. Top with the decorative top cookies. Serve the day the cookies are put together.

Storage: Store the cookies in an airtight container for up to 5 days if they haven't been sandwiched with the jam.

LEMON SHORTBREAD JAM SANDWICHES Omit the lavender and add the zest of 1 lemon to the cookie dough. Sandwich with the Black and Blue Jam (page 238).

These cookies are made with a Linzer cookie cutter that has 6 different cut out shapes for the centres.

Snacks and Treats

ANIMAL CRACKERS

Makes about 160 crackers, depending on the size of your cookie cutters

For animal crackers that will remind you of your own childhood, find the smallest and cutest animal cookie cutters you can. These are great to take into your kid's classroom on special occasions or for birthday party favours.

1½ cups (375 mL) all-purpose flour	½ cup (125 mL) butter, at room
1 cup (250 mL) arrowroot flour	temperature
½ tsp (2.5 mL) baking soda	2 eggs
¼ tsp (1 mL) fine sea salt	1 tsp (5 mL) pure vanilla extract
¾ cup (185 mL) granulated sugar	

PREHEAT THE OVEN to 325°F (160°C). Line 2 large baking sheets with parchment paper.

Sift the flour, arrowroot flour, baking soda and salt together in a medium bowl. Set aside.

Cream the sugar and butter together in the bowl of a stand mixer fitted with the paddle attachment. Add the eggs, one at a time, and mix until incorporated. Add the sifted dry ingredients and mix until the dough comes together and away from the sides of the bowl.

Divide the dough into 2 pieces. Wrap each piece in plastic wrap and refrigerate for 30 minutes.

Roll each piece of dough between 2 sheets of parchment paper until it is about ¼-inch (6 mm) thick. Cut out animal shapes with small animal cookie cutters and place on the prepared pans. Bake for about 15 minutes or until the animal crackers just start to turn golden around the edges. The animal crackers should be completely dry when they are at room temperature.

Storage: Store the crackers in an airtight container for up to 2 weeks.

SPOTTED ANIMAL CRACKERS You can also create "spotted" animal crackers by adding 1 Tbsp (15 mL) poppy seeds to the dry ingredients and then continuing with the recipe as above.

ARROWROOT FLOUR is easily digestible and its fine texture creates baked goods that have a fine crumb.

84

STRAWBERRY ICE POPS

Makes 5 or 6 ice pops

I try not to buy imported strawberries because there is something magical about the taste of local, freshly picked strawberries that I want to experience at least once a year. A bit of delayed gratification never hurt anyone. I urge you to make these ice pops with strawberries that are fresh from the field for maximum enjoyment. Kids of all ages will love them.

3 cups (750 mL) fresh strawberries, sliced

½ cup (125 mL) instant-dissolving sugar (also known as berry sugar)

¼ cup (60 mL) freshly squeezed lemon juice

COMBINE ALL OF the ingredients in the work bowl of a food processor or blender. Purée the mixture until smooth. Taste and add more sugar if necessary. Pour the mixture into individual ice pop moulds. Insert ice pop sticks into the moulds. Freeze until firm.

STRAWBERRY RHUBARB ICE POPS Fill the ice pop moulds with half Rhubarb-Vanilla Syrup (page 259) and half of the strawberry mixture above. Insert ice pop sticks into the moulds. Freeze until firm.

. . . .

CHOCOLATE PUDDING

Makes 8 servings

I like the fact that this pudding is made with cocoa powder instead of chocolate. It's easier to keep cocoa powder on hand than to keep chocolate in the cupboard (the same scenario as wine and vermouth, page 135). My kids love having this light and creamy pudding after school. The neighbour kids like it, too. Gavin and Ellen's friend Katie was contemplating coming over for a play date right off the school bus and she asked, "Did you make pudding today?"

3 cups (750 mL) whole milk, divided

1 cup (250 mL) whipping cream

1 cup (250 mL) granulated sugar

5 Tbsp (75 mL) cornstarch

¼ cup (60 mL) cocoa powder

pinch of fine sea salt

3 eggs

2 Tbsp (30 mL) butter

1 Tbsp (15 mL) pure vanilla extract

HEAT 2 CUPS (500 mL) milk and the cream in a large saucepan over medium heat until the mixture starts to steam. Reduce the heat to low.

Whisk the sugar, cornstarch, cocoa powder and salt together in a medium bowl. Add the remaining 1 cup (250 mL) of milk and the eggs and whisk until smooth.

Add a ladleful of hot milk to the egg mixture and quickly whisk together. Add another ladleful of hot milk and whisk again. Pour the whole chocolate mixture back into the saucepan with the warmed milk and cream. Cook, stirring constantly, over medium heat for about 5 minutes or until the mixture thickens to coat the back of a spoon.

Transfer the pudding into a clean bowl. Add the butter and vanilla extract and stir until the butter melts. Spoon the pudding into individual ramekins and serve warm, at room temperature or cold.

Storage: Keep the puddings, covered, in the refrigerator for up to 3 days.

VANILLA BEAN TAPIOCA PUDDING

Serves 8

I make this pudding quite often before Gavin and Ellen get home from school. Everyone has a snack and then I divvy up several portions for the kid's lunches (quickly, before anyone has a chance to eat it all). With any luck, I save the rest for an easy dessert that night.

7 cups (1.75 L) milk

⅔ cup (160 mL) granulated sugar

½ cup (125 mL) quick-cooking
    tapioca

3 eggs, lightly beaten

½ vanilla bean, split (see sidebar)

COMBINE ALL OF the ingredients in a large stockpot. Bring to a boil over medium heat, stirring constantly. Cook for 2 minutes and then remove from the heat. Cool the pudding and serve warm or at room temperature.

Storage: Store the puddings, covered, in the refrigerator for up to 3 days.

VANILLA BEANS are easier to find than ever. I store my vanilla beans in a canning quart jar with a mixture of vodka and pure vanilla extract. Often recipes will call for just the seeds inside the bean. After a vanilla bean has been split and seeded, place it back into the jar until needed.

PRETZEL CARAMELS

Makes about 6 dozen caramels

Caramels take a little more loving attention than most of the treats in this chapter but I encourage you to step out of your comfort zone and give it a shot. The crunch of the pretzels mixed with chewy caramel is highly addictive. Consider this a warning.

2½ cups (625 mL) broken pretzel sticks

1¾ cups (435 mL) granulated sugar

1½ cups (375 mL) evaporated milk

⅔ cup (160 mL) whipping cream

¾ cup (185 mL) corn syrup

¼ cup (60 mL) butter

1 tsp (5 mL) pure vanilla extract

LINE AN 11- × 17-INCH (28 × 42 cm) rimmed baking sheet (known as a jelly-roll pan) with parchment paper. Smear bits of butter on the pan to anchor the parchment paper to the pan perfectly.

Place the broken pretzel pieces in a sieve and shake out all of the pretzel dust. Sprinkle the broken pretzels evenly on the prepared pan. Set aside until needed.

Combine the sugar, evaporated milk and whipping cream in a large saucepan over medium-high heat. Bring to a boil without stirring. Reduce the heat to medium-low and add the corn syrup. Stir gently and often with a straight sided spoon or a wooden spoon. Clip a candy thermometer on the edge of the pan and continue cooking until the mixture reaches 230°F (110°C).

Add the butter to the bubbling caramel mixture and continue cooking until the mixture reaches 241°F (116°C). Stir constantly. Remove the saucepan from the heat and add the vanilla extract.

Carefully pour the caramel over the broken pretzel pieces. Quickly smooth the caramel out over the pretzels. Completely cool the caramel for at least 3 hours or overnight.

Cut the caramel into 1- × 2-inch (2.5 × 5 cm) pieces and wrap them in parchment paper squares or wax candy papers.

Storage: Keep the caramels in an airtight container for up to 1 month or in the freezer for up to 6 months.

A candy thermometer is a handy piece of equipment to have on hand. I prefer the inexpensive glass ones.

PEANUT BUTTER CHOCOLATE SQUARES

Makes about 24 squares

My biggest weakness every Hallowe'en are chocolate-covered peanut butter cups. It's in my best interest NOT to buy the chocolate bar variety bags that contain the iconic little orange packages (that doesn't mean I never buy them . . .). But everyone deserves a treat once in a while. Here is a homemade version that transports me immediately to the end of October.

2 cups (500 mL) icing sugar

1½ cups (375 mL) graham cracker crumbs

¾ cup (185 mL) butter, at room temperature

⅔ cup (160 mL) smooth peanut butter

8 oz (225 g) dark chocolate, chopped

LINE AN 8-INCH (20 cm) square baking pan with parchment paper. Set aside.

Combine the icing sugar and graham cracker crumbs in a medium bowl. Set aside.

Combine the butter and peanut butter in the bowl of a stand mixer fitted with the paddle attachment and mix until smooth. Add the dry ingredients slowly and blend until it all comes together. Press the mixture into the prepared pan. Cover and refrigerate for at least 1 hour.

Melt the chocolate in a heat-proof bowl set over a pan of simmering water. Pour the melted chocolate over the chilled peanut butter layer and smooth evenly. Refrigerate until the chocolate is set and then cut into 1-inch (2.5 cm) squares.

Storage: Keep the squares in an airtight container for up to 7 days. To keep the squares longer, store in the refrigerator for up to 3 weeks or freeze for up to 3 months.

Starters

Blue Cheese Dip   *94*

Warm Olives   *95*

Edamame Spread   *96*

Fresh Tortilla Chips with Guacamole   *98*

Grilled Bread   *100*

Retro Cheese Ball   *102*

Fresh Sesame Bread Sticks   *105*

Cheesy Spinach and Apple Squares   *106*

Prosciutto-Feta Bites   *107*

BLUE CHEESE DIP

Makes 1 cup (250 mL)

It is a well-documented fact at our house—if you put veggies out with this blue cheese dip, they will be eaten. For a dip that everyone will love, use a mild blue cheese such as Blue Benedictine from Quebec or a Danish Blue. This dip also goes well with Sunday Roast Beef Tenderloin (page 152) and Chicken Tenders (page 141), or really with just about anything from veggies to flank steak. It's also great thinned out as a salad dressing.

1 cup (250 mL) finely crumbled blue cheese

¼ cup (60 mL) Homemade Mayonnaise (page 250)

¼ cup (60 mL) sour cream

1 Tbsp (15 mL) fresh lemon juice

1 Tbsp (15 mL) thinly sliced fresh chives

¼ tsp (1 mL) fine sea salt

¼ tsp (1 mL) freshly ground black pepper

2 Tbsp (30 mL) milk, for adjusting the consistency to your taste

COMBINE ALL OF the ingredients in a medium bowl. Gradually add the milk until you reach the desired consistency. Refrigerate until needed.

Storage: The dip can be refrigerated in an airtight container for up to 3 days.

WARM OLIVES

Serves 4 to 6 people

I was at a party a few years ago and I stood in front of a plate of olives that had been warmed. I could have stood there all night, sipping wine and eating those delectable morsels. Slightly warming a pan of olives takes them to a whole new level. They shouldn't be hot, just warmed gently.

2 Tbsp (30 mL) extra-virgin olive oil   2 cups (500 mL) mixed olives

WARM THE OLIVE oil in a medium-sized cast-iron skillet over low heat. Add the olives. Occasionally give the pan a good shake and let the olives warm through, but they don't need to be hot. Serve straight from the pan or place the warm olives in a serving dish.

EDAMAME SPREAD

Makes about 1½ cups (375 mL)

Edamame are the young green soybeans that are popular in Japanese restaurants, where they are served in their husks. Edamame without the husks are now available in the frozen veggie section of most grocery stores. They remind me of fava beans without all the work.

2 cups (500 mL) frozen edamame
    beans
1 small garlic clove, minced
⅓ cup (80 mL) extra-virgin olive oil
¼ cup (60 mL) freshly squeezed
    lemon juice

½ tsp (2.5 mL) fine sea salt, or to
    taste
¼ tsp (1 mL) freshly ground black
    pepper

ADD THE FROZEN edamame to a saucepan of boiling water and cook for about 2 minutes, until tender. Rinse the edamame under cold water. Drain well.

Place the beans in a food processor with the garlic. Process briefly until the mixture is a coarse purée. Add the olive oil and lemon juice and pulse until combined. Season with salt and pepper. Serve at room temperature with Grilled Bread (page 100), Crostini or crackers.

Storage: The dip can be refrigerated in an airtight container for up to 3 days.

CROSTINI

Makes about 5 dozen crostini

Crostini are as close to perfect as a stale baguette can get. I firmly believe that everything tastes better on a crostini.

1 baguette
extra-virgin olive oil
fine sea salt

PREHEAT THE OVEN to 350°F (175°C). Thinly slice baguette. Brush each slice with olive oil and place on a baking sheet lined with parchment paper. Lightly sprinkle with fine sea salt. Bake for 10 minutes and then turn each slice over and bake for another 10 minutes, or until each slice is golden and crispy.

Let cool completely.

Storage: Keep the crostini in an airtight container at room temperature for up to 1 week.

FRESH TORTILLA CHIPS WITH GUACAMOLE

Serves 6

The idea of frying tortilla chips had never crossed my mind until my sister, Lori, mentioned that she had done them for a dinner party and that people totally loved them. I wasn't completely convinced. "Are you sure it's worth it?" I asked her. She insisted it was and, as usual, she was right!

neutral tasting oil, such as canola or peanut oil	1 package corn tortillas (I use a value pack that is 27 oz or 765 g)
	fine sea salt

POUR ABOUT 2 inches (5 cm) of oil into a large stockpot or fill a deep fryer according to the manufacturer's directions. Heat the oil to 375°F (190°C).

While the oil is heating up, cut the tortillas into 8 triangles each. This is the perfect size for eating with dips.

Place 8–10 tortilla pieces into the hot oil quickly and carefully. Move around to make sure they are all submerged for a short time. Cook the tortillas for approximately 2 minutes, until they stop steaming and appear golden.

Remove the chips from the oil and place them on a baking sheet lined with paper towels. Sprinkle generously with fine sea salt. Repeat the process until all of the tortilla pieces have been fried. Serve with guacamole.

Storage: These tortilla chips are best eaten the day they are made.

GUACAMOLE

Makes 3 cups

Last summer we met up with our friends Allana and Michael on Mermaid Island in the Thousand Islands. They docked their sailboat next to ours and we spent an idyllic weekend swimming, exploring and, of course, eating. For happy hour, I whipped up a big bowl of guacamole and although we didn't have freshly fried tortilla chips (quelle horreur!), we were a happy group nonetheless. I swear by limes and no garlic in my "guac".

4 ripe avocadoes

⅓ cup (80 mL) fresh lime juice (2–3 limes)

½ cup (125 mL) finely chopped green onions

½ cup (125 mL) chopped fresh cilantro

¾ tsp (4 mL) fine sea salt

SCOOP OUT THE flesh of the avocadoes and place in a large bowl. Add the lime juice and mash together until the mixture is more smooth than chunky. Add the green onions, cilantro and salt. Taste for seasoning using a tortilla chip (or whatever you are going to be eating the guacamole with). Serve at room temperature.

Storage: This dip is best eaten the day it's made.

VARIATIONS To add a bit of extra flavour, you could crumble ½ cup (125 mL) Macedonian feta cheese on top, or add ¾ cup (185 mL) diced fresh tomatoes or half of a finely minced jalapeño pepper into the mix.

GRILLED BREAD

Serves 4–6

In recent years, I have achieved a whole new appreciation for grilling breads. Whether we find ourselves camping, boating or hanging out at someone's cottage, there's always day-old bread around and I've discovered that it's perfect for grilling and serving with breakfast, lunch or dinner. The key is having really good butter on hand, such as Chive Flower Butter or Roasted Tomato Butter (page 118).

1 loaf good-quality bread of your
    choice

HEAT THE GRILL to about 350°F (175°C). Using a serrated knife, slice the loaf into approximately 1-inch (2.5 cm) slices. Toast the bread slices on the hot grill, being careful not to burn the bread too much. Dark grill marks are perfect, but a whole piece of charred bread is, as they say, toast.

Serve the grilled bread with Chive Flower Butter or a good-quality salted butter.

For grilling bread, I would recommend a baguette, ciabatta loaf or a rustic multigrain loaf. Any bread with a substantial crust will work marvellously.

CHIVE FLOWER BUTTER

Makes 1 cup

Chives are herbs that keep coming up in my garden year after year. It starts in the spring and I am sometimes still snipping it in October.

The blossoms that appear on chive plants in late spring/early summer taste like fresh onions. Pull the little blossoms off of the flower and make a batch of this butter or sprinkle them in a green salad. I make little logs of Chive Flower Butter and freeze them to use throughout the year.

6 or 7 chives with flowers
1 cup (250 mL) butter, at room temperature
½ tsp (2.5 mL) fine sea salt

PICK THE FLOWER petals off the stems of the chives. Save the chive stems for another use. Place the butter in the work bowl of a stand mixer fitted with a paddle attachment. Beat the butter until soft, about 1 minute. Add the salt and the chive flower blossoms. Beat until combined. Roll the butter into a log on a piece of parchment paper or wax paper. Refrigerate the roll of butter until firm.

Storage: Keep the butter wrapped in plastic wrap in the refrigerator for up to 2 weeks or freeze for up to 6 months.

RETRO CHEESE BALL

Serves 10

I was born in the early 70's and cheese balls were a standard for our generation. Somewhere along the way we forgot about the humble cheese ball but I assure you, this recipe will have you rethinking retro. Rolling this cheese ball in bright green pistachios really makes it stand out in a crowd. Serve with Crostini (page 96).

8 oz (240 g) cream cheese, at room temperature

3 cups (750 mL) grated sharp cheddar cheese

½ cup (125 mL) finely chopped green onions

¼ cup (60 mL) white wine

2 Tbsp (30 mL) finely chopped sun-dried tomato

2 tsp (10 mL) Worcestershire sauce

1 tsp (5 mL) minced garlic

½ tsp (2.5 mL) freshly ground black pepper

15 shakes hot sauce

⅓ cup (80 mL) pistachios, shelled and ground

COMBINE ALL OF the ingredients, except the nuts, in the work bowl of a stand mixer fitted with the paddle attachment until everything is thoroughly mixed. Scrape the mixture onto a piece of plastic wrap and form into a ball. Wrap the ball in the plastic wrap and chill in the refrigerator for at least 2 hours.

When you are ready to serve, unwrap the ball and gently roll in a dish of the ground pistachios. Place on a serving plate and surround with crackers, crostini or veggies.

Storage: The cheese ball can be kept, covered, in the refrigerator for up to 5 days.

FRESH SESAME BREAD STICKS

Makes 16 bread sticks

This is a great example of the no-knead bread doughs that have become so popular in the last number of years. Just mix everything together and let it rise. With this recipe, you can make as many bread sticks as you need at one time, while keeping the extra dough in the refrigerator. This also makes terrific pizza dough (page 148).

2 cups (500 mL) lukewarm water

½ cup (125 mL) extra-virgin olive oil, divided

1 Tbsp (15 mL) instant dry yeast

1 Tbsp (15 mL) fine sea salt

1 Tbsp (15 mL) granulated sugar

4 cups (1 L) all-purpose flour

¼ cup (60 mL) sesame seeds

1 Tbsp (15 mL) coarse sea salt

COMBINE THE WATER, ¼ cup (60 mL) olive oil, yeast, salt and sugar in a large bowl. Mix in the flour and stir until the flour is thoroughly incorporated. Cover loosely with plastic wrap. Allow the dough to rise at room temperature until it has at least doubled in size. The dough is ready to be used at this point or it can be covered and refrigerated until needed. The dough will last for at least 1 week in the refrigerator.

Line a large baking sheet with parchment paper.

If you are baking the bread sticks with freshly made dough that hasn't been refrigerated, divide the dough into quarters and then divide each quarter into 4 equal pieces. Lightly flour each piece and roll between your palms until each piece is a rope about 8 inches (20 cm) long. Lay each rope on the prepared pan. Allow the bread pieces to rise, uncovered, for about 30 minutes.

Preheat the oven to 425°F (220°C). Brush each breadstick with the remaining ¼ cup (60 mL) olive oil and sprinkle with the sesame seeds and coarse sea salt. Bake the bread sticks for about 15 minutes or until they start to turn golden around the edges. Remove from the oven and cool for at least 10 minutes before serving.

If you are baking the bread sticks with dough that has been refrigerated, follow the recipe as you would for fresh dough, except allow the shaped dough to rise for 1 hour before baking.

Storage: These bread sticks are at their best the day they are made.

CHEESY SPINACH AND APPLE SQUARES

Makes about 3 dozen squares

I have made these squares for many parties over the years—it's a great dish for a crowd. I was helping cater an event in Toronto for friends and a woman asked whether these squares had wheat in them. I told her that they did contain flour and I assumed that would be the end of it. Then I watched her eat more than her fair share of the warm cheesy squares throughout the afternoon. I guess she wasn't that worried about eating wheat!

3 eggs

1 cup (250 mL) milk

¼ cup (60 mL) melted butter

1 cup (250 mL) all-purpose flour

1 Tbsp (15 mL) baking powder

1½ tsp (7.5 mL) fine sea salt

½ tsp (2.5 mL) freshly ground black pepper

1 lb (500 g) sharp cheddar cheese, grated

4 oz (120 g) mozzarella cheese, grated

2 oz (60 g) parmesan cheese, grated

1 cup (250 mL) finely chopped and peeled apple (approximately 1 large apple)

½ cup (125 mL) finely chopped onion

1 lb (500 g) fresh baby spinach

PREHEAT THE OVEN to 350°F (175°C). Butter an 11- × 17-inch (28 × 42 cm) jelly-roll pan. Set aside.

Whisk the eggs, milk and melted butter together in a large bowl. Add the flour, baking powder, salt and pepper and mix thoroughly. Stir in the grated cheeses, apple, onion and spinach with a large spoon until combined.

Spread the spinach mixture into the prepared pan and smooth it out evenly. Bake for 30 minutes. Turn the broiler on and place the pan under the broiler for a few minutes until the top is golden. Slice into squares and serve warm.

This appetizer freezes well, either uncooked or cooked. If uncooked, don't thaw the spinach dish. Proceed with the recipe above and bake for an extra 5–10 minutes. If already cooked, reheat in a 325°F (160°C) oven for 20–30 minutes.

VARIATION If you need a gluten-free appetizer, simply substitute the all-purpose flour for an equal amount of a gluten-free flour mix. There are some great gluten-free baking flours available these days.

PROSCIUTTO-FETA BITES

Makes about 6 dozen bites

You only need to read the ingredient list to know this recipe is going to be good. The saltiness of the feta and prosciutto mingling with the fresh mint and red onion is so good, you may not be able to leave room for dinner. Have these made up ahead of time and pull them out of the refrigerator when needed. People will be singing your praises.

1 cup (250 mL) Macedonian feta cheese

½ cup (125 mL) cream cheese, at room temperature

½ cup (125 mL) chopped fresh mint

½ cup (125 mL) finely minced red onion

10 oz (300 g) good-quality prosciutto

2 Tbsp (30 mL) extra-virgin olive oil

BLEND THE FETA cheese and cream cheese in the bowl of a stand mixer fitted with the paddle attachment until combined. Add the mint and red onion and mix until incorporated.

The size of the prosciutto slices will dictate how to cut each piece. I cut each slice of prosciutto into 4 pieces that are about 2–3 inches (5–8 cm) long and 1-inch (2.5 cm) wide. Place about 1 tsp (5 mL) or so of the cheese mixture on the end of each piece of prosciutto and roll up evenly. Place the bites into a small shallow bowl and drizzle with olive oil. Refrigerate until needed.

These can be made up to 1 day in advance.

PROSCIUTTO is an Italian cured ham that is sliced very thin. It's widely available in grocery stores.

MACEDONIAN FETA is milder and creamier than other types of feta cheese.

Sides

Cabbage and Mashed Yukon Gold Potatoes   *110*

Shredded Potato Cake   *111*

Oven-Roasted Sweet Potato Wedges with
   Watercress Dip   *113*

Soft Polenta   *114*

Watsa's Rice Pilau   *115*

Cucumbers in Yogurt   *116*

Soda Bread with Dried Cherries   *117*

Corn on the Cob with Roasted Tomato Butter   *118*

Pan-Fried Brussels Sprouts with Maple Syrup
   and Bacon   *121*

Roasted Cauliflower   *122*

Baked Carrots with Horseradish   *123*

Broccoli with Cheddar Cheese Sauce   *125*

CABBAGE AND MASHED YUKON GOLD POTATOES

Serves 6

For mashed potatoes, I like using Yukon Gold potatoes, warm milk and lots of butter. The addition of thinly sliced cooked cabbage to mashed potatoes is known as Colcannon, a classic Irish comfort food. Serve with Meatloaf (page 129), Sunday Roast Beef Tenderloin (page 152) or Chicken with Dried Plums and Green Olives (page 135).

3 lb (1.5 kg) Yukon Gold potatoes, peeled

1 medium green cabbage

1 cup (250 mL) whole milk

½ cup (125 mL) butter

½ cup (125 mL) finely sliced green onions

1½ tsp (7.5 mL) fine sea salt

½ tsp (2.5 mL) freshly ground black pepper

CUT THE POTATOES into chunks and boil in salted water until they are tender. Drain the potatoes and leave them in the pan, uncovered, so that any remaining water can evaporate.

While the potatoes are cooking, remove the outer leaves of the cabbage and cut into quarters. Cut out the hard ribs of each quarter and thinly slice the cabbage. You will probably have about 8 cups (2 L) of sliced cabbage. Bring a second large pot of water to a boil and add the sliced cabbage. Cook for about 10 minutes, until tender. Drain well.

Heat the milk and butter in a small saucepan until the butter is melted.

Put the potatoes through a ricer (or mash the potatoes using your favourite method) and add the warm milk and butter. Mix thoroughly. Fold in the cabbage and green onions. Season with salt and pepper. Serve warm.

SHREDDED POTATO CAKE

Serves 4–6

This crispy round of potatoes is known as rösti. When we ask my dad what he'd like for dinner when he comes to visit, this is always tops on his list. To make a meal of this, serve with fresh chives and smoked salmon or trout. No wonder he visits so often.

2 lb (1 kg) Yukon Gold potatoes

1 tsp (5 mL) fine sea salt

¼ tsp (1 mL) freshly ground black
  pepper

¼ cup (60 mL) olive oil, divided

¼ cup (60 mL) butter, divided

sour cream or Greek yogurt, for
  serving

PEEL THE POTATOES and shred them either in a food processor fitted with the shredder attachment or with a hand grater. Place the shredded potatoes in a large bowl and sprinkle with salt and pepper. Toss to combine.

Heat a large cast-iron skillet over medium-high heat. Add 2 Tbsp (30 mL) olive oil and 2 Tbsp (30 mL) butter. When the butter has melted, press all of the shredded potatoes into the pan and smooth the top. Cover with a lid and cook over medium heat for about 10–15 minutes, or until the bottom of the potatoes has turned dark golden and crispy.

Loosen the edges of the potato cake with a knife. Remove the pan from the heat and place a large plate upside down on top of it. Carefully flip the potato cake onto the plate and set to the side. Return the pan to the stove over medium heat. Heat the remaining 2 Tbsp (30 mL) of olive oil and 2 Tbsp (30 mL) butter in the pan. Slide the potato cake back into the sizzling pan with the uncooked side on the bottom and cover with a lid.

Cook the potato cake for another 10–15 minutes. Remove the lid and cook for another few minutes, until the bottom is golden and crispy like the top. Serve the potato cake directly from the cast-iron skillet with sour cream.

VARIATION To make individual potato cakes, follow the recipe above but instead of adding all of the shredded potatoes to the pan at once, place ½ cup (125 mL) portions into the pan, leaving enough space between the cakes to flip them. These will take about 10–15 minutes to cook. Place finished potato cakes on a baking sheet lined with paper towel and keep them warm in a 250°F (120°C) oven.

OVEN-ROASTED SWEET POTATO WEDGES WITH WATERCRESS DIP

Serves 4

It's hard to say what I like better, the sweet potato wedges or the watercress dip! The wedges are crispy on the outside and soft and sweet on the inside. We never have leftovers. The watercress dip is good with almost everything. Try it as part of a party buffet with crudité or kettle chips or serve with Seared Salmon (page 142).

2 lb (1 kg) sweet potatoes, peeled	1 tsp (5 mL) fine sea salt
¼ cup (60 mL) cornstarch	¼ tsp (1 mL) freshly ground black
½ cup (125 mL) coconut oil, melted	pepper

PREHEAT THE OVEN to 400°F (200°C). Line a large baking sheet with parchment paper.

Slice the sweet potatoes into thin wedges and place in a large bowl. Dust the wedges with cornstarch. Pour the coconut oil over the sweet potatoes and toss with the salt and pepper. Place on the prepared baking sheet in a single layer.

Roast the sweet potatoes for about 20 minutes. Flip the sweet potatoes over and return the pan to the oven for another 15 minutes or so. When the wedges start to darken around the edges and are cooked through, remove the sweet potatoes from the oven. Serve hot with the Watercress Dip.

COCONUT OIL is a healthy oil that seems to be creeping into my cooking more and more.

WATERCRESS DIP

Makes about 2 cups (500 mL)

I'm lucky to have a number of people in my life who know a lot about food and my cousin Beth is one of the best. When she makes a suggestion, like the idea for this dip, I know I better sit up and listen.

1 cup (250 mL) Homemade Mayonnaise (page 250)
½ cup (125 mL) sour cream
1 bunch watercress

4 tsp (20 mL) freshly squeezed lemon juice
1 Tbsp (15 mL) finely chopped red onion
1 Tbsp (15 mL) Dijon mustard
½ tsp (2.5 mL) fine sea salt
½ tsp (2.5 mL) freshly ground black pepper

Combine all of the ingredients in the work bowl of a food processor and process until smooth.

Storage: Keep this dip in an airtight container in the refrigerator for up to 3 days.

. . . .

SOFT POLENTA

Serves 6

Polenta is essentially a cornmeal porridge, but don't let that description put you off. I like polenta so much that when I see it on a menu, it almost doesn't matter to me what the main course is. Serve with Braised Lamb Shanks (page 160) or Basted Beer-Can Chicken (page 165).

6 cups (1.5 L) Chicken or Veggie Stock (pages 251 and 252)	¾ tsp (4 mL) fine sea salt, or to taste
1½ cups (375 mL) coarse ground polenta	1 cup (250 mL) grated parmesan cheese
	¼ cup (60 mL) butter

BRING THE STOCK to a boil over high heat in a saucepan. Add the polenta and salt and reduce the heat to medium-low. Stir frequently for about 10–12 minutes, or until the polenta is thickened and soft. Add the parmesan cheese and butter, combine thoroughly and serve immediately.

Storage: Keep leftovers in an airtight container in the refrigerator for up to 4 days.

If the leftover polenta is quite firm after it's been refrigerated, I form it into little patties and fry them in olive oil in a cast-iron skillet.

WATSA'S RICE PILAU

Serves 8

My friend Shaila's mom, Margaret Watsa, is wonderful at cooking all things Indian. It helps that she's been married to Shaila's dad Ranjan, who was born and raised in Hyderabad, India, for over 40 years. Known as rice pilau, this Indian dish is a staple at their home. It's now a staple at mine, too. Serve with My Favourite Chicken Curry (page 136).

¼ cup (60 mL) grape seed oil

2 cups (500 mL) thinly sliced onions

one 4-inch (10 cm) piece cinnamon
  stick

8 whole cloves

8 whole green cardamom pods

1 tsp (5 mL) minced garlic

1 tsp (5 mL) finely grated ginger

1 tsp (5 mL) cumin seeds

4 cups (1 L) Chicken Stock (page 251)

2 cups (500 mL) frozen mixed veggies

2 Tbsp (30 mL) fresh lemon juice

2 tsp (10 mL) fine sea salt

2 cups (500 mL) uncooked basmati
  rice, rinsed in cold water

1 cup (250 mL) chopped cilantro

½ cup (125 mL) chopped fresh mint

HEAT THE OIL in a large Dutch oven or stockpot over medium heat. Add the sliced onions and cook over medium-low heat for about 30 minutes, or until the onions are caramelized. Reduce the heat to low and add the cinnamon stick, cloves, cardamom pods, garlic, ginger and cumin seeds and cook for a few minutes.

Add the stock, veggies, lemon juice and salt to the stockpot and bring the mixture to a boil. Add the rinsed rice and return to a boil. Reduce the heat to low, stir well and cover the pot. Cook on low for about 15 minutes. Remove the pot from the heat and stir in the chopped cilantro and mint. Serve warm.

Storage: Keep leftovers in an airtight container in the refrigerator for up to 4 days.

VARIATION Margaret's original recipe called for frozen mixed veggies but if you want to substitute fresh, add ¾ cup (185 mL) small-dice carrots, ¾ cup (185 mL) chopped green beans and ½ cup (125 mL) corn kernels. Add to the pot in place of the frozen mixed vegetables.

CUCUMBERS IN YOGURT

Serves 6

This cucumber dish made regular appearances at family dinners when I was growing up. This is a year-round recipe that goes well with almost any main course. Cucumbers in Yogurt could win an Oscar for best supporting side dish.

2 English cucumbers, skins on

1 tsp (5 mL) fine sea salt

¼ cup (60 mL) plain whole-milk yogurt (not strained)

2 Tbsp (30 mL) fresh lemon juice

1 Tbsp (15 mL) fresh dill

1 Tbsp (15 mL) apple cider vinegar

½ tsp (2.5 mL) granulated sugar

THINLY SLICE THE cucumbers. Place the slices in a large bowl and sprinkle with salt, tossing to combine. Cover the bowl and refrigerate for 1 hour.

Drain the cucumbers and press out the excess liquid.

In a medium bowl, stir together the yogurt, lemon juice, dill, vinegar and sugar. Combine the yogurt mixture with the prepared cucumbers. Refrigerate, covered, until ready to serve.

Storage: The cucumbers will keep, covered, in the refrigerator for up to 3 days.

SODA BREAD WITH DRIED CHERRIES

Makes 1 loaf

This is a seriously easy bread to whip up before any meal. Dried cherries go really well with any savoury dish. We love dried cherries so much, I sometimes wonder if it might be cheaper in the long run for us to buy a cherry farm.

4 cups (1 L) all-purpose flour

3 Tbsp (45 mL) granulated sugar

1 tsp (5 mL) baking soda

1 tsp (5 mL) fine sea salt

¼ cup (60 mL) cold butter, cut into
   small pieces

1¾ cups (435 mL) buttermilk

1 egg

1 cup (250 mL) dried cherries

PREHEAT THE OVEN to 375°F (190°C). Line a baking sheet with parchment paper.

Whisk together the flour, sugar, baking soda and salt in a large bowl. Add the cold butter. Work the butter into the flour with your fingertips until the butter is almost all incorporated.

In a separate bowl, beat the buttermilk and egg together. Add the liquid to the dry ingredients. Give it a few turns with a wooden spoon and add the cherries. Continue to mix the dough until most of the flour has been incorporated.

Turn the dough out onto a lightly floured board and knead it a few times into a large round loaf. Place the loaf on the prepared pan and make a few cuts into the top of the loaf with a serrated knife.

Bake for about 45 minutes, or until a wooden skewer comes out of the middle clean.

Cool on a baking rack and serve warm or at room temperature, slathered with butter.

Storage: This bread is best eaten the day it's made.

VARIATION If you don't have dried cherries on hand, you can use raisins, currants or even chopped dried apricots.

CORN ON THE COB WITH ROASTED TOMATO BUTTER

Serves 4

I remember my mom, in her white nurse's uniform, coming home after her shift at the hospital with bags of fresh produce from the vegetable stands around southern Essex County. She would call for us to get the corn shucked and she would slice perfectly ripe tomatoes while we waited for the corn water to boil. There is a certain time each summer when it's possible to happily eat only what is grown in your proverbial backyard. This recipe proves that theory.

8 ears fresh sweet corn, husked   extra-virgin olive oil

ON THE GRILL: Brush each cob of corn with a small bit of olive oil. Place the corncobs on the grill and turn occasionally, as the kernels start to char. Remove from the grill and serve warm with Roasted Tomato Butter (page 120).

BOILED: Bring a large pot of water to a boil. Add the corn to the pot and set a timer for 5 minutes. Remove the corn from the water and serve warm with Roasted Tomato Butter (page 120).

ROASTED TOMATO BUTTER

Makes 1 cup (250 mL)

This butter goes well with pretty much anything you can think of, especially Corn on the Cob (page 118) and Grilled Bread (page 100).

2 cups (500 mL) cherry tomatoes, halved
1 tsp (5 mL) fine sea salt
½ cup (125 mL) butter, at room temperature
¼ cup (60 mL) finely chopped fresh chives

PREHEAT THE OVEN to 400°F (200°C). Line a baking sheet with parchment paper.

Place the halved tomatoes on the baking sheet, seed side up. Sprinkle generously with sea salt. Roast for 30 minutes, or until the tomatoes start to wrinkle and darken around the edges. Set aside to cool.

Place the roasted tomatoes and butter in a food processor. Process briefly, until the mixture is almost smooth. Scoop the butter mixture into a clean bowl and fold in the chives. Taste for seasoning. Serve the butter at room temperature.

Storage: Store leftover butter in an airtight container in the refrigerator for up to 1 week.

Sides

PAN-FRIED BRUSSELS SPROUTS WITH MAPLE SYRUP AND BACON

Serves 4-6

This recipe has Thanksgiving written all over it. Brussels sprouts are one of those foods that people think of when asked what their least favourite food is. But if they were having them served up like this, I doubt there would be as many naysayers. Serve with Seared Salmon (page 142) or Braised Lamb Shanks (page 160).

6 slices bacon, diced

½ cup (125 mL) diced onion

4 cups (1 L) thinly sliced Brussels
  sprouts, approximately 1 lb (500 g)

1 large tart apple, peeled, cored and
  chopped

¾ cup (185 mL) apple cider

½ cup (125 mL) maple syrup

½ tsp (2.5 mL) fine sea salt

¼ tsp (1 mL) freshly ground black
  pepper

FRY THE BACON in a large cast-iron skillet until crisp. Remove the bacon and set aside, leaving the bacon grease in the pan. Add the onion and cook until softened. Add the Brussels sprouts, chopped apple, apple cider, salt and pepper. Cook over medium-low heat for about 20 minutes, or until the Brussels sprouts have really softened. Add the maple syrup and cook over low heat for another 5 minutes until the whole mixture starts to caramelize. Taste for seasoning. Serve hot.

The easiest way to slice Brussels sprouts is to put them through the food processor with the slicer attachment.

ROASTED CAULIFLOWER

Serves 4

Roasting cauliflower is a great way to get kids interested in eating their veggies. It becomes unbelievably sweet and if I leave it out on the counter before dinner, the kids eat it like its candy. Now that's a habit you can feel good about!

1 large head cauliflower

¼ cup (60 mL) extra-virgin olive oil

½ tsp (2.5 mL) fine sea salt

¼ tsp (1 mL) freshly ground black pepper

PREHEAT THE OVEN to 400°F (200°C). Line a large baking sheet with parchment paper and set aside.

Slice the cauliflower into thin pieces. Toss in a large bowl with the olive oil, salt and pepper. Spread the cauliflower out on the prepared baking sheet. Roast for about 30 minutes or until the edges start to darken and the larger pieces are cooked through.

Remove from the oven and serve hot.

BAKED CARROTS WITH HORSERADISH

Serves 6

Baked carrots don't sound enticing to you? You've got to try this recipe. The flavour of fresh carrots (the ones with tops on usually taste the best) in a light creamy horseradish sauce is totally delish. Serve with Seared Salmon (page 142), Sunday Roast Beef Tenderloin (page 152) or Ribs with Chuck's Barbecue Sauce (page 158).

2 lb (1 kg) fresh carrots	¼ tsp (1 mL) freshly ground black
1 cup (250 mL) Homemade	pepper
Mayonnaise (page 250)	½ cup (125 mL) Fresh Bread Crumbs
¼ cup (60 mL) finely diced onion	(page 71)
2 Tbsp (30 mL) horseradish	pinch of sweet paprika
½ tsp (2.5 mL) fine sea salt	2 Tbsp (30 mL) finely chopped parsley

PREHEAT THE OVEN to 375°F (190°C). Butter an 8-inch (20 cm) square baking dish.

Peel the carrots and trim the ends.

Bring a large pot of salted water to a boil. Add the prepared carrots and boil for about 5 minutes or until tender. Reserve ¼ cup (60 mL) of cooking water from the pot.

Cut the carrots into narrow strips and arrange in the prepared baking dish.

Combine the reserved cooking water, mayonnaise, diced onion, horseradish, salt and pepper. Pour the mixture over the carrots. Sprinkle with the bread crumbs. Sprinkle with paprika and parsley.

Bake for 20 minutes. Serve hot. If you are making the dish in advance, cover the dish before baking and refrigerate until needed. Bake, uncovered, at 375°F (190°C) for 30 minutes or until heated through.

BROCCOLI WITH CHEDDAR CHEESE SAUCE

Serves 4

We always knew it was a special dinner when my mom served cheese sauce with broccoli. In fact, cheese sauce was one of the first things I learned to make well and now I'm teaching my kids to make it. Do I need to mention that the better quality the cheddar cheese, the better the cheese sauce? Consider this a friendly reminder. If you're a fan of this classic combination, you'll also love the Broccoli-Cheddar Soup (page 70).

(page 70)

2 Tbsp (30 mL) butter

2 Tbsp (30 mL) all-purpose flour

1 cup (250 mL) whole milk

2 cups (500 mL) grated sharp cheddar cheese

¼ tsp (1 mL) fine sea salt

pinch freshly ground black pepper

1 large head of broccoli (or 2 smaller heads), trimmed and cut into florets

MELT THE BUTTER in a medium saucepan over medium heat. Add the flour and cook for 1–2 minutes, stirring constantly. Whisk the milk into the butter mixture and continue cooking until the sauce is smooth and thick. Add the grated cheese, salt and pepper. Taste for seasoning. Keep warm until needed.

Bring a large pot with 1-inch (2.5 cm) of water in the bottom to a boil. Place a steamer basket in the pot and fill with the broccoli florets. Cover the pot and let the broccoli steam for about 3 minutes. Serve the broccoli hot with the cheese sauce on the side.

Weeknight Suppers

Beef Stroganoff   *128*

Meatloaf   *129*

Cottage Pie   *130*

Lamb Burgers with Yogurt-Cucumber Spread   *132*

Chicken with Dried Plums and Green Olives   *135*

My Favourite Chicken Curry   *136*

Sailboat Chicken   *140*

Chicken Tenders with Honey-Mustard
   Dipping Sauce   *141*

Seared Salmon   *142*

Mixed Mushroom Risotto   *144*

White Bean and Tomato Linguini   *145*

Goat Cheese and Herb Ravioli   *146*

Homemade Pizza   *148*

BEEF STROGANOFF

Serves 6–8

I remember my mom making beef stroganoff quite often when I was growing up. My cousin Beth sent me a recipe for beef stroganoff a few years ago and it seems she had the same memories as I did (which makes sense because our mothers are identical twins!). When Stroganoff is made well it is the perfect blend of beef, mushrooms and a savoury cream sauce. You're bound to start getting requests after making it once.

2 lb (1 kg) beef strip loin, cut into
  1-inch (2.5 cm) strips
2 Tbsp (30 mL) all-purpose flour
1 tsp (5 mL) fine sea salt
½ tsp (2.5 mL) freshly ground black
  pepper
2 Tbsp (30 mL) grape seed oil
2 Tbsp (30 mL) butter
2 cups (500 mL) chopped onions

1 tsp (5 mL) smoked paprika
8 cups (2 L) halved or quartered
  mushrooms (a mix of wild and
  domestic mushrooms is nice)
2 Tbsp (30 mL) Worcestershire sauce
2 cups (500 mL) Chicken Stock (page
  251), or beef stock
2 cups (500 mL) sour cream
¼ cup (60 mL) finely chopped parsley

TOSS THE SLICED beef with the flour, salt and pepper. Set aside.

Heat the oil in a large cast-iron pan or Dutch oven over medium-high heat. Add the beef slices, cooking them in batches if there isn't enough room. Remove the cooked beef to a clean plate and set aside. Do not wipe the pan clean.

Reduce the heat to medium-low and melt the butter in the pan. Add the chopped onions and smoked paprika to the pan and cook until the onions are soft, about 5 minutes. Add the mushrooms and cook gently for 5 minutes. Add the Worcestershire sauce and the stock and bring to a boil. Simmer for a few minutes until the sauce has started to thicken.

Return the beef to the sauce and add the sour cream and chopped parsley.

Serve over hot Basmati Rice (page 53) or hot-buttered egg noodles.

. . . .

MEATLOAF

Serves 6

We like having meatloaf for dinner and then in sandwiches the next day. The boys in Gavin's class are particularly interested when he pulls a meatloaf sandwich out of his lunch bag. One of the boys once said to Gavin, "Your mom must be a great chef!" High praise indeed.

2 Tbsp (30 mL) olive oil	2 eggs
1 cup (250 mL) finely minced onions	1 tsp (5 mL) fine sea salt
½ cup (125 mL) finely grated carrots	½ tsp (2.5 mL) freshly ground black
½ cup (125 mL) finely minced celery	pepper
3 cloves garlic, minced	½ tsp (2.5 mL) chili powder
2 lb (1 kg) ground beef	¾ cup (185 mL) Chili Sauce with
1 lb (500 g) ground pork	Fruit (page 248) or ½ cup (125 mL)
¾ cup (185 mL) Fresh Bread Crumbs	ketchup
(page 71)	

PREHEAT THE OVEN to 350°F (175°C). Line a baking sheet with parchment paper.

Heat the olive oil in a large cast-iron skillet over medium-low heat. Add the onions, carrots, celery and garlic and cook the vegetables for about 5 minutes, just until they are soft but not browning. Remove the pan from the heat and let the vegetables cool.

Combine the cooled vegetables, ground meats, bread crumbs, eggs, salt, pepper and chili powder in a large bowl and mix together using clean hands. Don't over mix or the meatloaf will be tough.

Dump the meat mixture out onto the prepared baking sheet and form into a wide loaf shape. Spoon the chili sauce or ketchup over the meatloaf. Bake for about 1½ hours or until the meatloaf is cooked through the middle.

Let the meatloaf sit for about 10 minutes before slicing it into 1-inch (2.5 cm) thick pieces. Serve hot with more chili sauce and Cabbage and Mashed Yukon Gold Potatoes (page 110).

MEATBALLS Make the mixture above and gently form into 2-inch (5 cm) balls. Place on a baking sheet lined with parchment paper and bake for about 30 minutes or until the meatballs are cooked through. Serve with pasta or mashed potatoes.

. . . .

COTTAGE PIE

Serves 6

There is a hillside near our house that is home to a small group of Scottish Highland cattle, the very furry, horned cows that originated in Scotland. Apparently the owners are forever having people stop to take pictures of the majestic beasts and I happen to be one of them. These cows have acres of grassy fields to wander around and they seem to be living the best possible life a cow could ask for.

I'm very conscious about where I buy meat, how it was raised, and I try very hard not to waste the meat we do buy. That's why I love recipes like this one—you can use ground beef that you've bought specifically for the recipe or use the leftovers from a roast beef dinner the night before. And don't let the name fool you, this beefy version of shepherd's pie can be eaten anywhere.

¼ cup (60 mL) olive oil, divided

1 cup (250 mL) chopped onions

1 cup (250 mL) peeled and chopped carrots

1 cup (250 mL) chopped celery

1 Tbsp (15 mL) fine sea salt, divided

1 tsp (5 mL) smoked paprika

1 tsp (5 mL) freshly ground black pepper, divided

5 lb (2.5 Kg) Yukon Gold potatoes, peeled

1¼ cups (310 mL) whole milk

½ cup (125 mL) butter

1½ cups (375 mL) grated sharp cheddar cheese

½ cup (125 mL) finely chopped green onions

2 lb (1 kg) ground beef or leftover Sunday Roast Beef Tenderloin (page 152), cut into small pieces

¼ cup (60 mL) red wine

1 Tbsp (15 mL) tomato paste

1 Tbsp (15 mL) Worcestershire sauce

1 Tbsp (15 mL) soy sauce

PREHEAT THE OVEN to 350°F (175°C). Lightly butter a 9- × 13-inch (23 × 33 cm) baking dish and set aside.

Heat 2 Tbsp (30 mL) olive oil in a large saucepan over medium heat. Add the onions, carrots and celery and cook over medium-low heat for about 5 minutes until the veggies start to soften. Add 2 tsp (10 mL) salt, smoked paprika, and ½ tsp (2.5 mL) pepper to the veggies and continue cooking the veggies for another 5 minutes or so. Place the vegetable mixture into a bowl and return the stockpot to the stove. Don't wipe clean.

While the vegetables are cooking, cut the potatoes into chunks and boil in salted water until they are tender. Drain the potatoes and leave them in the pan, uncovered, so that any water remaining evaporates. Heat the milk and butter in a small saucepan until the butter is melted.

Put the potatoes through a ricer (or mash the potatoes using your favourite method) and add the warm milk and butter. Mix thoroughly. Fold in the grated cheddar cheese and the green onions. Season with salt and pepper. Keep warm.

Heat the remaining 2 Tbsp (30 mL) olive oil in the saucepan over medium heat. Add the beef (the ground beef or leftover roast beef), remaining 1 tsp (5 mL) salt, and ½ tsp (2.5 mL) pepper to the saucepan and cook until the meat is crumbled and cooked through. Add the red wine, tomato paste, Worcestershire sauce and soy sauce to the meat mixture. Cook for a few minutes over medium-low heat to allow the flavours to mingle. Place the vegetable mixture back into the saucepan and combine well. Taste for seasoning. Remove from the heat.

Place the meat mixture in the bottom of the prepared pan and spread evenly. Scoop even dollops of the mashed potatoes onto the beef mixture and smooth it over, creating an even top. Bake the cottage pie for about 25 minutes or until the meat mixture starts to bubble up and the mashed potatoes start to turn golden. Serve hot.

LAMB BURGERS WITH YOGURT-CUCUMBER SPREAD

Serves 4

Every fall we buy a butchered lamb to stock our freezer with for the winter. The farmer, Adrian, raises very few lambs each year but lucky for us we have a standing order. Whenever I visit his CSA farm (see page two for more info on CSA farms), it's a little slice of paradise and I truly hate to leave. For several years, their farm was home to a very lazy black pig named Roxanne, who happened to be blind. She didn't do a whole lot but everyone loved her. I think this speaks well of Adrian and his family.

As for these burgers, speaking from experience, you may want to double this recipe if you know your family is hungry.

FOR THE BURGERS

1 lb (500 g) ground lamb

½ cup (125 mL) cooked Basmati Rice
  (page 53)

½ cup (125 mL) chopped fresh mint

1 egg yolk

1 garlic clove, finely chopped

1 tsp (5 mL) ground cumin

¾ tsp (4 mL) fine sea salt

½ tsp (2.5 mL) smoked paprika

¼ tsp (1 mL) freshly ground black
  pepper

FOR THE YOGURT-CUCUMBER SPREAD

¾ cup (185 mL) Greek yogurt

¾ cup (185 mL) finely diced
  cucumber

1½ Tbsp (22.5 mL) extra-virgin
  olive oil

¼ tsp (1 mL) fine sea salt

TO SERVE

4 fresh burger buns

1 batch Yogurt-Cucumber Spread, or
  your favourite store-bought tzatziki

½ cup (125 mL) crumbled feta cheese

4 thin tomato slices, or a handful
  of sliced cherry tomatoes

4 thin red onion slices

4 lettuce leaves

FOR THE BURGERS: Combine all of the burger ingredients together in a large bowl. Divide the mixture into 4 portions. Gently form them into balls, and press down on them to form patties that are about 1-inch (2.5 cm) thick.

Heat the grill to about 400°F (200°C). Cook the patties on the grill, turning once, until browned on both sides and cooked through, about 4–5 minutes per side.

FOR THE YOGURT-CUCUMBER SPREAD: Combine the yogurt, cucumber, olive oil and salt and mix well. Set aside until needed or cover and refrigerate for up to 3 days ahead of time.

TO SERVE: Serve each burger on a bun with a dollop of Yogurt-Cucumber Spread, a lettuce leaf, an onion slice, a tomato slice and 2 Tbsp (30 mL) feta cheese.

CHICKEN WITH DRIED PLUMS AND GREEN OLIVES

Serves 6

The first time I had this dish, my friend Shaila made it for a girls' weekend in Tofino, British Columbia. The chicken was marinated the day before we left and it became a memorable dinner for our first night on the outer reaches of Vancouver Island. Served with creamy mashed potatoes, a leafy green salad and a view of the ocean, we were a very happy bunch.

Even if you aren't a fan of green olives and capers, leave them in. When they are cooked in with the chicken and the marinade, they are mouth-wateringly delicious. This recipe is so much more than the sum of its parts.

FOR MARINATING THE CHICKEN

2½–3½ lb (1.25–1.75 kg) bone-in, skin-on chicken thighs

1 cup (250 mL) pitted prunes

½ cup (125 mL) green olives

⅓ cup (80 mL) red wine vinegar

⅓ cup (80 mL) extra-virgin olive oil

¼ cup (60 mL) dried oregano

¼ cup (60 mL) capers with 1 Tbsp (15 mL) juice

2½ Tbsp (37.5 mL) minced garlic

1½ tsp (7.5 mL) fine sea salt

¾ tsp (4 mL) freshly ground black pepper

3 bay leaves

FOR COOKING THE CHICKEN

¼ cup (60 mL) brown sugar

½ cup (125 mL) vermouth (see sidebar)

¼ cup (60 mL) finely chopped parsley

COMBINE THE CHICKEN thighs with all of the marinade ingredients in a large bowl. Cover and refrigerate overnight. If you are taking the chicken somewhere the next day, divide the chicken and marinade into large resealable plastic bags.

When you are ready to cook the chicken, preheat the oven to 350°F (175°C). Arrange the chicken in a single layer in a large baking dish, dividing the marinade evenly between them.

Sprinkle the chicken with brown sugar and pour the vermouth over everything. Bake for 1–1½ hours basting frequently every 15 minutes or so. When the chicken is finished, sprinkle with parsley and serve hot.

VERMOUTH is a fortified wine, sometimes used in martinis, that has been enhanced with herbs and other botanicals. I always keep a bottle or two of vermouth in the cupboard for those times that I want to add wine to a recipe and we don't have any.

MY FAVOURITE CHICKEN CURRY

Serves 6

I started making curries after a trip to India (see details on page 139). One of our host families was Bharath Kumar and his wife, Anu. Their kitchen was in a separate building off to the side of their house and the cooking that came out of there was unbelievably good. Every morning they had fresh buffalo milk delivered from their rice farm which was a few miles away. It was made into butter for cooking. They also had a vegetable seller who came up to a special window in the house and Anu bought fresh cilantro and other ingredients from him daily. It was a real lesson to me about eating and cooking with the freshest food possible.

⅓ cup (80 mL) grape seed oil

2 cups (500 mL) chopped onions

5 garlic cloves

1-inch (2.5 cm) piece of ginger, peeled
  and chopped

1 red-hot chili pepper, seeded and
  finely chopped

2 green cardamom pods

1 large cinnamon stick

5 whole cloves

5 black peppercorns

2 Tbsp (30 mL) ground coriander

2 Tbsp (30 mL) ground cumin

¼ tsp (1 mL) turmeric

2 cups (500 mL) diced or crushed
  tomatoes (canned)

3–4 lb (1.5–1.8 kg) bone-in, skinless
  chicken thighs

½ cup (125 mL) water

1½ tsp (7.5 mL) fine sea salt

¼ cup (60 mL) sour cream

juice of ½ lemon

1 bunch fresh cilantro, chopped and
  divided

thick plain whole-milk yogurt

HEAT THE OIL in a large saucepan or Dutch oven over medium heat. Process the onions in a food processor and add to the saucepan. Brown over medium heat, stirring frequently, until the onions are a deep golden brown, about 15 minutes. Stir in 1–2 Tbsp (15–30 mL) of water to keep the onions from burning. Do this as often as you need to.

Meanwhile, without rinsing the bowl of the food processor, process the garlic, ginger and chili pepper until finely minced. Set aside until needed.

Once the onions have browned, add the ginger-garlic mixture and sauté for a minute or so, adding a little more water if needed to prevent sticking.

Add all of the spices and continue to brown for another 2 minutes. Add the diced or crushed tomatoes and their juices and cook until the solids separate from the oil, about 5 minutes.

Add the chicken thighs and cook on medium-high heat, about 5 minutes. Add the water and salt. Cover and simmer for about 45 minutes, or until the chicken is cooked through.

Continued . . .

MY FAVOURITE CHICKEN CURRY (*continued*)

Add a little more water if needed during the cooking process. The curry should have the consistency of thick gravy.

Remove the chicken thighs from the curry mixture. Remove the whole spices carefully. Let the chicken cool on a plate and when it is cool enough to handle, remove the meat from the bones and return the meat to the curry mixture. Cook for another 10–15 minutes over medium-low heat.

Before serving, add the sour cream and stir it in thoroughly. Add the freshly squeezed lemon juice and half of the chopped cilantro. Use the remaining cilantro to serve at the table. Serve with Watsa's Rice Pilau (page 115) or cooked Basmati Rice (page 53) and plain yogurt.

I have a couple of tips you should keep in mind when making a chicken curry, or any spicy food for that matter. Firstly, the fresher your spices, the better the flavour of your dish. When I have time, I toast cumin and coriander seeds in a small cast-iron pan and then grind them myself. If you don't use these spices very often, smell them to make sure they are still fresh enough to give lots of flavour. My other tip is to remember to count the whole spices that you are adding to the pot—whatever you put in should come out before serving.

There are a few spices that I buy in larger quantities—cinnamon, cumin, coriander, chili powder. The rest of the spices tend not to be used as often and I buy them in smaller quantities—cardamom, ginger, nutmeg, cloves, etc. I try to keep enough stock that I don't run out but not so much that I have to dispose of a lot after it's been around too long.

MIXED MUSHROOM RISOTTO

Serves 4

Risotto should be considered (good) fast food. The key to making it happen quickly is having Chicken Stock (page 144) on hand. Everything else can be prepped quickly and in stages, making it the ultimate quick meal.

At our local farmers' market, there is a farmer that sells a variety of beautiful mushrooms throughout the summer. Keep your eyes peeled for your own local "mushroom guy"!

¼ cup + 2 Tbsp (60 mL + 30 mL) butter

8 cups (2 L) sliced mushrooms, combination of portobello, oyster, brown, shiitake or your favourites

½ tsp (2.5 mL) fine sea salt

1 clove garlic, minced

7 cups (1.75 L) Homemade Chicken Stock (page xx) (approx)

2 Tbsp (30 mL) olive oil

1 cup (250 mL) chopped onions

1½ cups (375 mL) Arborio rice

½ cup (125 mL) vermouth

1 cup (250 mL) freshly grated parmesan cheese

¼ cup (60 mL) finely chopped fresh chives

MELT ¼ CUP (60 mL) butter in a large cast-iron skillet over medium-high heat. Add the mushrooms, reduce the heat to medium, and cook for about 5 minutes. Sprinkle with salt. Add the minced garlic and cook for another 5 minutes or so, until the mushrooms have reduced in size and really start to smell good.

Bring the chicken stock to a boil. Reduce to a simmer and keep hot until needed.

Meanwhile, heat the remaining 2 Tbsp (30 mL) butter and olive oil together in a large saucepan over medium heat. Add the chopped onions and cook until softened, about 5 minutes. Add the rice and stir until the rice is thoroughly coated with the butter and oil. Add the vermouth to the rice and stir. When the vermouth has almost evaporated, start adding the chicken stock to the rice ½ cup (125 mL) at a time, stirring constantly with a wooden spoon. Add more stock after the liquid has started to evaporate. The rice should be kept moist at all times but you don't want to flood it with stock. This process should take 15–20 minutes.

Add the cooked mushrooms to the risotto. Fold in the grated parmesan cheese. Sprinkle with the fresh chives and serve hot.

My favourite way to eat leftover risotto is to form it into patties and fry it in olive oil.

WHITE BEAN AND TOMATO LINGUINI

Serves 4

Here's a pasta dish that relies on ingredients that we all have in our cupboards. I only started puréeing the sauce because my children were anti-white bean for a while (ok, they still might be) but I love the "creaminess" of the sauce when it's put through the food processor.

¼ cup (60 mL) olive oil

2 cups (500 mL) chopped onions

1 Tbsp (15 mL) minced garlic

one 28 oz (796 mL) can diced
   tomatoes, with their juices

one 15 oz (425 mL) can white beans
   (navy or cannellini are great),
   drained and rinsed

¾ tsp (4 mL) fine sea salt

¼ tsp (1 mL) freshly ground black
   pepper

one 12 oz (340 g) package linguini
   noodles

extra-virgin olive oil, to taste

¾ cup (185 mL) grated parmesan
   cheese, plus extra for serving

½ cup (125 mL) finely chopped fresh
   parsley, plus extra for serving

HEAT THE OLIVE oil in a large skillet or wide saucepan over medium heat. Add the chopped onions and cook for about 5 minutes or until the onions are softened. Add the garlic and continue cooking for a few minutes. Add the tomatoes, white beans, salt and pepper and simmer over medium-low heat for about 10 minutes.

While the tomato-bean mixture is cooking, bring a large stockpot of salted water to a boil. Add the pasta and cook according to the manufacturer's directions. Drain the pasta, reserving some of the pasta water to thin the sauce if necessary.

Blend the tomato-bean mixture in a food processor until smooth. Return the sauce to the pan and add the parmesan cheese and fresh parsley. Add some of the reserved pasta water to thin the sauce enough so that it has the consistency of a thick cream. Toss the hot pasta with the tomato-bean sauce. Add a ladleful of pasta water to the pan if the sauce is still too thick.

Divide the pasta into serving bowls and drizzle with a little extra-virgin olive oil. Sprinkle with the extra parmesan cheese and chopped parsley. Serve hot.

GOAT CHEESE AND HERB RAVIOLI

Serves 4

You might be thinking that this doesn't seem like a quick dinner option but it really is. Using won-ton wrappers and putting the filling together ahead of time makes things even easier and I always get helpers to work the assembly line.

1 lb (500 g) goat cheese
1 cup (250 mL) ricotta cheese
½ cup (125 mL) finely chopped basil
½ cup (125 mL) finely chopped chives
½ tsp (2.5 mL) fine sea salt
¼ tsp (1 mL) freshly ground black
  pepper

one 14 oz (398 g) package small
  won-ton wrappers
1½ cups (375 mL) All-Season Tomato
  Sauce (page 247) or your favourite
  tomato sauce
extra-virgin olive oil, for drizzling

BLEND THE GOAT cheese, ricotta, basil, chives, salt and pepper in the bowl of a stand mixer fitted with the paddle attachment. Taste for seasoning.

Lay out several won-ton wrappers on a flat surface. Place a 2 tsp (10 mL) blob of the goat cheese mixture on the centre of each wrapper. Using your finger, moisten the edges of one wrapper at a time with water. Place a won-ton wrapper on top of the goat cheese mixture and press with your fingers so the ravioli are airtight. Try not to trap too much air inside the ravioli. Continue with the rest of the wrappers and filling. You will end up with about 25 ravioli.

Warm the tomato sauce in a small saucepan over medium-low heat.

Bring a large pot of water to a boil. Cook the ravioli in the boiling water (in a couple of batches if your pot isn't large enough) for 3 minutes, until the wrapper is cooked through. Remove the cooked ravioli to a colander.

Divide the cooked ravioli into 4 bowls and serve with the hot tomato sauce and a drizzle of olive oil.

Depending on how full you fill each ravioli, you may have extra filling. The goat cheese mixture makes for a great spread for crackers, Crostini (page 96) and veggies.

HOMEMADE PIZZA

Makes 8 individual pizzas

The key to making this recipe a weekday supper is having the dough and the pizza sauce made in advance. Keeping the dough ready to go in the refrigerator means that all you have to do is divvy it up and you're ready for a Friday night pizza party. We make pizzas at birthday parties or when we have other families coming over for a visit. Everyone loves to decorate their own pizza.

1 full recipe of dough from Fresh Sesame Bread Sticks (page 105), made up ahead of time	16 fresh basil leaves
4 tsp (20 mL) extra-virgin olive oil	16 pieces thinly sliced sweet soppressata salami
1 cup (250 mL) Homemade Pizza Sauce (page 246)	1 small red onion, thinly sliced
1 lb (500 g) ball of mozzarella cheese	½ cup (125 mL) green olives, finely chopped (optional)

PLACE A PIZZA stone in the oven, if you have one (see sidebar, page 151). Preheat the oven to 450°F (230°C). Cut out eight 9-inch (23 cm) square pieces of parchment paper.

Divide the dough into 8 pieces. Start stretching the dough with your hands or use a rolling pin until the dough is quite thin. If the dough keeps shrinking back up, leave it for 5 minutes and try again. Place the pieces of dough on the parchment paper squares. Use a fork to prick holes in the dough. Drizzle about ½ tsp (2.5 mL) of olive oil on each round of dough and spread it around with your fingers. Continue to stretch the dough until it is the desired thickness. If you want to keep track of whose pizza is whose, now is a good time to write your name on a corner of each parchment paper.

Top with a thin layer of pizza sauce. Use the sauce sparingly—too much sauce makes for soggy pizza. Divide the grated mozzarella cheese among the pizzas. Place 2 basil leaves and 2 pieces of the soppressata on each pizza. Sprinkle with a few slices of red onion and 1 Tbsp (15 mL) green olives.

Place the pizzas on the baking stone. Bake for about 10 minutes, until the pizzas start to turn golden around the edges. The pizzas are ready when the cheese has melted and the bottoms are a light golden brown.

Remove from the oven and serve hot.

VARIATION If you don't have a baking stone, place a baking sheet in the oven for about 10 minutes before you are ready to bake the pizzas. Carefully remove the baking sheet from the oven and slide the unbaked pizzas onto the pan. You may only be able to cook a couple at a time but they will cook in a similar way to a stone.

On the other hand, if you do decide to invest in a baking stone, don't chintz out. You get what you pay for in this department.

Weekend Dinners

Sunday Roast Beef Tenderloin   *152*
Cabbage Rolls   *154*
Winter Meat Pies   *156*
Ribs with Chuck's Barbecue Sauce   *158*
Braised Lamb Shanks   *160*
Chicken and Dumplings   *162*
Basted Beer-Can Chicken   *165*
Perch-in-a-Basket with Tartar Sauce   *166*
Stuffed Shells   *169*

SUNDAY ROAST BEEF TENDERLOIN

Serves 8

When my brother-in-law, Jake, suggested that I cook a beef tenderloin at 250°F (120°C), I was skeptical. But he was so right. The meat was cooked through evenly from the outer crust to the inside. The rub that I used added little hits of flavour in every bite and I wouldn't be exaggerating when I say that it's so good, you'll be shooing people away from the leftovers.

¼ cup (60 mL) coarse sea salt

¼ cup (60 mL) granulated sugar

1 Tbsp (15 mL) dried chili flakes

1 tsp (5 mL) freshly ground black pepper

3 lb (1.5 kg) trimmed beef tenderloin

PLACE THE SALT, sugar, chili flakes and pepper in a food processor and grind for about 30 seconds or until the chili flakes are finely ground.

Rub the whole beef tenderloin with the salt-sugar rub. Set the beef on a rack and place the rack on a large baking sheet lined with parchment paper. Let the beef sit at room temperature for about 1 hour.

Preheat the oven to 250°F (120°C). Place the beef in the oven and roast for about 1½ hours. Check the internal temperature of the beef—135°F (57°C) gives you a nice pink medium. Remove the beef from the oven and let it sit under a piece of tin foil for 15 minutes.

Slice the beef thinly and serve with the Horseradish Cream.

HORSERADISH CREAM

Makes ¾ cup (185 mL)

¾ cup (185 mL) sour cream

2 Tbsp (30 mL) prepared horseradish

2 Tbsp (30 mL) finely chopped chives

Combine all of the ingredients and refrigerate until needed. Serve with roast beef.

CABBAGE ROLLS

Serves 6

Who knew that cabbage rolls could be so good? These are not your run-of-the-mill, canned tomato soup–covered cabbage rolls. These are covered in a slightly sweetened homemade tomato sauce making them super moist and super good. Definitely worthy of second helpings, cabbage rolls are a great meal to make on a rainy day.

FOR THE CABBAGE LEAVES

1 large head of green cabbage

1 Tbsp (15 mL) fine sea salt

FOR THE SAUCE

3 Tbsp (45 mL) extra-virgin olive oil

2 Tbsp (30 mL) minced garlic

2 Tbsp (30 mL) brown sugar

2 Tbsp (30 mL) Worcestershire sauce

1 tsp (5 mL) hot chili flakes, dried

¼ tsp (1 mL) freshly ground black pepper

8 cups (2 L) All-Season Tomato Sauce (page 247)

FOR THE FILLING

1 lb (500 g) ground turkey

1 lb (500 g) ground beef

1 cup (250 mL) finely chopped yellow onions

2 cups (500 mL) Basmati Rice, cooked (page 53)

¼ cup (60 mL) fresh basil, chopped

2 Tbsp (30 mL) olive oil

1 Tbsp (15 mL) minced garlic

2 large eggs

2 tsp (10 mL) fine sea salt

1 tsp (5 mL) smoked paprika

½ tsp (2.5 mL) freshly ground black pepper

FOR THE CABBAGE LEAVES: Remove the 4 or 5 outermost leaves from the cabbage. Run under cold water and set aside.

Fill a large stockpot about two-thirds full of water. Bring the water to a boil. Add the salt.

Carefully place the whole head of cabbage in the boiling water and cook about 2 minutes, until the leaves start to lift away from the head. Using tongs and a sharp paring knife, cut the leaves away as they become soft and pliable. Set the leaves on a baking sheet to cool.

Continue cooking the leaves of the cabbage, layer by layer. Do not overcook the leaves or they will be difficult to work with.

You will need 12–14 large leaves. When you have reached the inner part of the cabbage, discard it or save for another use.

FOR THE SAUCE: Heat the olive oil in a large saucepan over low-medium heat. Cook the minced garlic for about 2 minutes, until it starts to soften but not colour. Add the remaining ingredients to the saucepan and bring to a boil over medium-high heat. Reduce the heat and simmer over low heat for 20 minutes. Set aside until needed.

FOR THE FILLING: Combine all of the filling ingredients in a large bowl until well mixed.

TO MAKE THE ROLLS: Preheat the oven to 325°F (160°C).

In a large roasting pan, ladle 1½ cups (375 mL) of the tomato sauce evenly in the bottom.

Using your hands, mould ½ cup (125 mL) of the filling mixture into a roll. Place the roll of filling at the base end of a boiled cabbage leaf. Roll the cabbage part way and fold in the sides. Continue rolling the leaf and place, seam side down, in the roasting pan. Roll enough cabbage rolls to cover the bottom of the roasting pan.

With a sharp paring knife, make a 1-inch (2.5 cm) slit in the top of each roll. Ladle about 2 cups (250 mL) of tomato sauce over the cabbage rolls.

Use the remaining cabbage leaves and filling to finish rolling the cabbage rolls and place on top of the first layer. Be sure to make slits in this layer, as well. The slits allow the tomato sauce to drip into the cabbage rolls, making them moist and very flavourful.

Ladle all of the remaining sauce on top of the whole pan. Cover everything with the outer raw cabbage leaves that were set aside at the beginning. Cover with a lid or tin foil.

Bake for 3 hours. Remove the cabbage leaves from the top. Serve hot.

. . . .

WINTER MEAT PIES

Makes 4 pies

This recipe came to me by way of my friend Janette. She was given the recipe from a woman whose husband was an executive at the Heinz plant in Leamington, Ontario for many years, hence the addition of "Heinz Ketchup" in the recipe. It may seem like a big recipe if you don't have a large family, but by freezing three of the pies for later you've just gained three delicious dinners to have in the near (or not so near) future.

I consider this recipe to be a southern Ontario version of the French Canadian tourtière. It's now our Christmas Eve dinner tradition. Let it snow, let it snow, let it snow!

2 lb (1 kg) ground pork

1 lb (500 g) ground beef

2 cups (500 mL) chopped onion

1 Tbsp (15 mL) minced garlic

½ cup (125 mL) Heinz ketchup, or your favourite ketchup

2 Tbsp (30 mL) Worcestershire sauce

2 Tbsp (30 mL) beef bouillon concentrate (or 2 beef bouillon cubes)

2 tsp (10 mL) fine sea salt

1 tsp (5 mL) freshly ground black pepper

1–1½ lb (500–750 g) peeled potatoes, cut into small chunks (about 4 or 5 medium-sized potatoes)

2 cups (500 mL) green peas (fresh or frozen)

8 discs Flaky Pie Dough (page 222)

1 egg

2 Tbsp (30 mL) milk

PLACE THE GROUND pork and beef in a large pot, mashing it down. Add water to the pot, to just cover the meat, about 3 cups (750 mL). Add the chopped onion, minced garlic, ketchup, Worcestershire sauce, beef bouillon, salt and pepper. Bring to a boil and then simmer, uncovered, for 2 hours, stirring occasionally.

While the meat is cooking, cover the potato chunks with cold water in a large saucepan. Bring to a boil and cook for about 20 minutes, or until tender. Remove from the heat, drain and mash the potatoes coarsely.

Skim any excess fat off the top of the meat after 2 hours, but don't take it all out. Add the mashed potatoes and peas. Cool completely in the refrigerator.

To put the meat pies together, roll out 4 discs of pie dough for four 9-inch (23 cm) pie plates. Divide the meat mixture evenly among the pie shells and level off. Cover with a top crust and flute the edges. Cut a decorative piece of holly and berries out of some extra pastry dough and place in the middle of the crust. Poke some slits in the top crust to allow steam to escape, and either bake immediately or double wrap in plastic wrap and freeze until needed.

To bake, preheat the oven to 450°F (230°C). Whisk the egg and milk together and brush the pastry with the egg wash. Place the pie in the oven and immediately turn the temperature down to 375°F (190°C). Bake for 45 minutes to 1 hour, until the pie crust is golden brown and the meat mixture is bubbling. Your house will smell scrumptious.

If you are baking a frozen pie, don't thaw it before baking. Brush with egg wash and add an extra 15 minutes to the baking time.

VARIATION My husband Alan grew up with tourtière made by his mom, Ellen. She included the more typical spices—cinnamon and cloves—in her tourtières.

RIBS WITH CHUCK'S BARBECUE SAUCE

Serves 4-6

There are two types of barbecue sauces—a thick red sauce and a thin vinegar-based sauce. This is a great example of the latter. My dad, Chuck, was given this recipe from our friends in Mississippi when I was a kid. I've revised that old favourite and according to my dad, it's almost as good as the original. Thanks dad.

2 cups (500 mL) apple cider vinegar

1 cup (250 mL) grape seed oil

¼ cup (60 mL) finely chopped onion

2 Tbsp (30 mL) fine sea salt, plus more for seasoning

2 cloves garlic, finely chopped

1 tsp (5 mL) crushed red pepper

½ tsp (2.5 mL) freshly ground black pepper

3 racks pork back ribs, about 5–6 lb (2.2–2.7 kg)

COMBINE ALL OF the ingredients except the ribs in a medium saucepan. Place over medium-high heat and bring to a boil. Turn down the heat immediately and continue simmering the sauce for 10 minutes. Let cool and use the marinade immediately or keep refrigerated in an airtight container for up to 2 weeks.

Heat the grill to about 375°F (190°C). Season the ribs with salt and pepper. Place the ribs on the grill and cook for about 10 minutes on each side, basting with the marinade as you go. Continue cooking the ribs for another 20 minutes or so, preferably over indirect heat. The more marinade you brush on the ribs, the more flavourful the ribs will be. Remove the ribs from the grill and cut into pieces. Serve warm.

If you are using a charcoal grill, add some mesquite chips to the charcoal for some delicious smoke.

BRAISED LAMB SHANKS

Serves 4

Lamb shanks need a long, slow braise until they are fall-off-the-bone ready. Serve with Soft Polenta (page 114) for the best cold-weather dinner imaginable.

4 lamb shanks, about 1 lb (500 g) each	1 cup (250 mL) diced onion
1 tsp (5 mL) fine sea salt	2 Tbsp (30 mL) minced garlic
½ tsp (2.5 mL) freshly ground black pepper	2 Tbsp (30 mL) fresh thyme leaves
	3 cups (750 mL) Chicken Stock (page 251) or beef stock
¼ cup (60 mL) olive oil	
1 cup (250 mL) diced carrot	1 Tbsp (15 mL) cornstarch
1 cup (250 mL) diced celery	3 Tbsp (45 mL) water

PREHEAT THE OVEN to 300°F (150°C). Heat an oven-safe Dutch oven or large stockpot over medium-high heat.

Pat the shanks dry with a paper towel. Season the meat generously with salt and pepper. Pour the olive oil into the hot pan. Place the shanks in the pan, being careful to avoid oil splatters. Brown the meat very well on all sides. Remove the shanks from the pan and set aside until needed.

Discard all but about 1 Tbsp (15 mL) oil from the pan. Place the pan back over medium heat and add the diced vegetables. Add the garlic and thyme leaves after the vegetables have had a good chance to start cooking, about 5 minutes.

Add the stock to the pan. Place the shanks in the pan so that they are all evenly covered with stock. Bring the mixture to a boil. Cover the pan with a tight fitting lid or aluminum foil and bake in the oven for about 3 hours, or until the meat is tender enough to be pulled off the bones easily.

Remove the lamb shanks. Strain the liquid and set the vegetables aside.

Reduce the liquid over medium-high heat for 5 minutes. Mix the cornstarch and water together in a small bowl. Whisk the cornstarch mixture into the liquid gradually until the sauce is thick enough to coat the back of a spoon—a nice gravy consistency. Return the lamb and vegetables back to the pan and coat everything in the sauce.

Serve hot over Soft Polenta (page 114) with Pan-Fried Brussels Sprouts with Maple Syrup and Bacon (page 121).

CHICKEN AND DUMPLINGS

Serves 4

This dish reminds me of my time spent in the hills of east Tennessee attending college. Under the guise of getting an education, I learned more about the joys of Southern cooking than I did in any of the classes I was enrolled in. The South does comfort food really well and this stick-to-your-ribs dinner is not only delicious, it can go straight from the oven to the table.

FOR THE CHICKEN

2 Tbsp (30 mL) grape seed oil

2 lb (1 kg) boneless, skinless chicken
  breasts, cut into bite-sized pieces

1½ tsp (7.5 mL) fine sea salt, divided

¼ tsp (1 mL) freshly ground black
  pepper

2 Tbsp (30 mL) butter

2 cups (500 mL) chopped onions

2 cups (500 mL) chopped carrots

1 cup (250 mL) finely chopped celery

¼ cup (60 mL) all-purpose flour

3 cups (750 mL) Chicken Stock
  (page 251)

FOR THE DUMPLINGS

1½ cups (375 mL) all-purpose flour

2 tsp (10 mL) baking powder

½ tsp (2.5 mL) fine sea salt

¾ cup (185 mL) milk

¼ cup (60 mL) butter

FOR THE CHICKEN: Warm the oil in a large Dutch oven (with a lid) over medium-high heat. Place the chicken pieces in the pan and season with 1 tsp (5 mL) salt and pepper. Cook until the chicken is no longer pink. Remove the chicken to a clean plate and set aside.

Lower the heat to medium and add the butter. Cook the onions, carrots and celery for about 5 minutes, until the veggies have softened. Add the flour to the pot and continue stirring for a few minutes, giving the flour time to cook. Whisk in the chicken stock and remaining ½ tsp (2.5 mL) salt and bring the mixture to a boil. Return the chicken pieces to the pot. Lower the heat to a simmer and continue cooking for about 20 minutes.

FOR THE DUMPLINGS: Combine the flour, baking powder and salt in a medium bowl. In a small saucepan, heat the milk and butter together until the butter has mostly melted. Pour the warm milk mixture over the flour and stir together until it forms a smooth dough.

Drop clumps of the dough on the simmering stew, leaving space between the dumplings. Cover the pot and simmer the dish for about 15 minutes, until the dumplings have cooked through. Serve hot.

We have a charcoal grill that is easy enough to use (I could kiss whoever invented the charcoal chimney) for most grilling. However, you really have to be on your A-game to get a beer-can chicken done perfectly over charcoal. We usually have to add a second chimney of hot coals to the barbecue to get us through the cooking process. A fool-proof gas barbecue is much easier to negotiate.

BASTED BEER-CAN CHICKEN

Serve 4–6

The secret to this moist, mouth-watering beer-can chicken comes from the beer that steams inside the chicken and the basting sauce that is brushed on the chicken every 5 minutes or so while the chicken is cooking.

Beer-can chicken is made easier with a contraption that can be bought specifically for the job. Metal arms keep the can of beer and chicken in place over a small pan that holds it all steady. You can make beer-can chickens without this contraption. Simply place the beer-can on a metal pan and continue with the recipe. Just be careful the chicken doesn't fall over!

½ cup (125 mL) soy sauce

½ cup (125 mL) butter

one 13 fl oz (355 mL) can beer, cider
or ginger ale

1 whole chicken, 3–4 lb (1.5–1.8 kg)

1 tsp (5 mL) fine sea salt

PREHEAT THE BARBECUE to about 375°F (190°C).

Heat the soy sauce and butter together in a small saucepan. Set aside.

Pour out half of the beer from the can. Place the can of beer in the centre of the beer-can-chicken holder, if using.

Salt the inside cavity of the chicken. Place the chicken on the beer-can-chicken holder or on the can of beer set on a sturdy metal baking dish. Place on the hot grill and brush with the soy marinade. Close the lid and cook the chicken for about 1–1½ hours, depending on the size of the chicken and the heat of the barbecue. Baste the chicken with the soy-butter sauce every 5 minutes or so throughout the cooking time.

The chicken is done when the joints are very loose and the juices run clear. Carve the chicken up into 8 pieces and serve hot.

> **SOY-BASTED ROAST CHICKEN** Roast a 3–4 lb (1.5 kg–1.8 kg) chicken in a 300°F (150°C) oven for 3 hours. Baste with the soy-butter sauce (see recipe above) every 10 minutes. This may seem like a lot of work but you'll be well rewarded for your efforts.

PERCH-IN-A-BASKET WITH TARTAR SAUCE

Serves 4–6

I love everything about perch. Catching it, cooking it, eating it—what's not to love? I recently found out that a friend of mine from Harrow even had it for her wedding dinner. I wish I had thought of that!

1½ cups (375 mL) all-purpose flour
1 Tbsp (15 mL) fine sea salt
½ tsp (2.5 mL) freshly ground black
  pepper
2 eggs
¼ cup (60 mL) milk

1½ cups (375 mL) finely ground
  saltine crackers (about 1½ sleeves
  of saltines)
vegetable oil for frying
2 lb (1 kg) fresh yellow perch fillets
  (skin on is fine)

COMBINE THE FLOUR, salt and pepper in a bowl. Whisk the eggs and milk together in a second bowl. Place the finely crushed saltines in a third bowl. Place the bowls in this order next to the stove where you will be cooking the fish.

Heat about 2 inches (5 cm) of oil in a large saucepan over medium-high heat. Use a deep-fry thermometer if you have one—the ideal temperature is 375°F (190°C)—or check that the oil is ready by dropping a small piece of bread into the hot oil to see if it bubbles right away. Preheat the oven to 250°F (120°C).

Dredge each fillet in the flour mixture, egg mixture and finally in the crushed saltines. Carefully place 3 or 4 fillets in the hot oil. Turn the fillets once they have turned a dark golden on one side. When the pieces are done, remove from the oil and place on a baking sheet lined with paper towels.

Place the finished fish in the oven to keep warm and continue frying the rest of fillets. Serve hot with Tartar Sauce (page 168).

SHRIMP-IN-A-BASKET Inspired by an old roadhouse tavern called The Meadows near the shores of Lake Erie, Shrimp-in-a-Basket used to be a glamorous dinner for us kids to order on a Saturday night. To go that route, follow the recipe above using 2 lb (1 kg) of black tiger shrimp instead of the perch.

PERCHWICHES Leftover pieces of fried perch are perfect for making "perchwiches". Slice a soft roll in half and layer Homemade Mayonnaise (page 250) or Tartar Sauce (page 168), 2 or 3 pieces of warmed up Perch-in-a-Basket, a slice of ripe tomato and a piece of green leaf lettuce. A good reason to plan for leftovers!

Saltine crackers are a staple in our house. They make excellent pre-seasoned crumbs. For this recipe, grind the saltines in a food processor for a minute or two, until the crumbs are smooth and fine.

TARTAR SAUCE

Makes 1½ cups (375 mL)

I honestly think tartar sauce can make or break a fish dinner. This recipe is quick and delicious and an absolute must if you are serving fried fish. If more restaurants took a few minutes to put together a tartar sauce like this, I'm sure it would increase their business!

1 cup (250 mL) Homemade Mayonnaise (page 250)
½ cup (125 mL) finely chopped dill pickle
¼ cup (60 mL) finely chopped chives
1 Tbsp (15 mL) fresh lemon juice
1 tsp (5 mL) Worcestershire Sauce

COMBINE ALL OF the ingredients in a medium bowl and mix thoroughly. Serve immediately or cover and refrigerate until needed.

Storage: The sauce will keep in the refrigerator for up to 5 days.

STUFFED SHELLS

Serves 6

This recipe is from my friend Isa who is one of the most talented cooks on the Niagara peninsula, and it is Italian comfort food at its best. With parents who emigrated from Italy, Isa was exposed to home cooking and vegetable gardens that many of us only dream about. She was destined for a career in food and for that, we are thankful.

FOR THE SAUCE

2 Tbsp + 2 Tbsp (30 mL + 30 mL) extra-virgin olive oil

2 tsp (10 mL) minced garlic

6 cups (1.5 L) All-Season Tomato Sauce (page 247)

2 tsp (10 mL) granulated sugar

1 tsp (5 mL) fine sea salt

½ tsp (2.5 mL) freshly ground black pepper

¼ tsp (1 mL) dried oregano

¼ cup (60 mL) finely chopped fresh basil

FOR THE FILLING

1 ½ lb (750 g) ricotta cheese

2 eggs

¾ cup (185 mL) parmesan cheese

½ cup (125 mL) finely chopped fresh parsley

½ cup (125 mL) finely chopped fresh basil

¾ tsp (4 mL) fine sea salt

¼ tsp (1 mL) freshly ground black pepper

TO ASSEMBLE

one 12 oz (340 g) package jumbo pasta shells

1 Tbsp (15 mL) fine sea salt

1 lb (500 g) ball of mozzarella cheese, grated

extra-virgin olive oil

FOR THE SAUCE: Heat 2 Tbsp (30 mL) olive oil in a large saucepan over low-medium heat. Cook the minced garlic for about 2 minutes, until it starts to soften but not colour. Add the remaining ingredients, except the fresh basil, to the saucepan and bring to a boil over medium-high heat. Reduce the heat and simmer over low heat for 20 minutes. Add the fresh basil and set aside until needed.

Continued . . .

STUFFED SHELLS (*continued*)

FOR THE FILLING: Combine the ricotta cheese, eggs, parmesan cheese, fresh herbs, salt and pepper. Set aside until the shells are ready.

Bring a large stockpot of salted water to a boil. Cook the pasta, according to the manufacturer's directions, until the shells are al dente. Drain the shells thoroughly.

Preheat the oven to 350°F (175°C). To assemble, spread about 1 cup (250 mL) of the sauce on the bottom of a 9- × 13-inch (23 × 33 cm) baking pan. Fill each shell with a generous Tbsp (15 mL) of the ricotta filling. Place the filled shells in the pan. Cover with the remaining tomato sauce. Sprinkle with freshly grated mozzarella cheese and drizzle with the remaining 2 Tbsp (30 mL) olive oil.

Cover the pan with aluminum foil and bake for 30 minutes. Uncover the pan and bake for another 10–15 minutes. Let the stuffed shells sit for a few minutes and serve hot.

This is a great dish to serve to a crowd. Double or triple the recipe accordingly.

THE DIRTY DISHES PLAYLIST

When you spend a lot of time in the kitchen, dirty dishes are inevitable. Dishes are my least favourite task and I find it helps to have some upbeat music on hand to get me through. I keep my iPod loaded with music (and podcasts) and this is one of my favourite 70's inspired playlists.

Bond Street — BURT BACHARACH · *More Than a Woman* — BEE GEES · *House of Bamboo* — EARL GRANT · *Use Ta Be My Girl* — THE O'JAYS · *Soul Bossa Nova* — QUINCY JONES & HIS ORCHESTRA · *Fantasy* — EARTH, WIND & FIRE · *A Swingin' Safari* — BERT KAEMPFERT & HIS ORCHESTRA · *Wonderwall* — THE MIKE FLOWERS POPS · *Rise* — HERB ALPERT · *Boy from Ipanema* — PEGGY LEE · *Give Me the Night* — GEORGE BENSON · *Lady Love* — LOU RAWLS

Everyday Desserts

Strawberry Shortcakes   *174*

Double Vanilla Pound Cake   *176*

Caramelized Pear Gingerbread Cake   *177*

Raspberry Cream Cheese Brownies   *179*

Peach-Blueberry Cobbler   *181*

Bubble-Gum Ice Cream   *182*

(Moira) Sanders Hot Fudge Sauce   *184*

Walnut-Spice Icebox Cookies   *185*

Stamped Shortbread Cookies   *187*

Malted Milk Cookies   *188*

Apple Strudel   *191*

STRAWBERRY SHORTCAKES

Makes 8 individual shortcakes

This is the best use of red, ripe strawberries. Ever.

2 cups (500 mL) all-purpose flour

2 Tbsp (30 mL) granulated sugar, plus more for sprinkling on the shortcakes

1 Tbsp (15 mL) baking powder

½ tsp (2.5 mL) fine sea salt

½ cup (125 mL) very cold butter, cut into small pieces

1 cup (250 mL) whipping cream, plus more for brushing on the shortcakes

6 cups (1.5 L) sliced fresh strawberries

1½ cups (375 mL) whipped cream, lightly sweetened

PREHEAT THE OVEN to 425°F (220°C). Line a baking sheet with parchment paper.

Combine the flour, sugar, baking powder and salt in the bowl of a stand mixer fitted with a paddle attachment. Add the butter and mix until the butter starts to incorporate into the flour, about 30 seconds.

Add the cream and continue blending until the dough comes together. Dump the dough out onto a lightly floured surface and gently roll the dough into a rectangle about 1½ inches (4 cm) thick. Fold the dough up like a letter and roll the dough into a rectangle again. Repeat the process again 3 times.

After the dough has been shaped into a rectangle for the fourth time, cut it into 8 even squares and place the squares on the prepared baking sheets. Brush with more whipping cream and sprinkle generously with granulated sugar. Bake for about 15 minutes, or until the bottom edges start to turn golden. Cool on a baking rack.

Serve the shortcakes, split in half, with fresh berries and whipped cream.

Storage: The shortcakes are best eaten the day they are made.

DOUBLE VANILLA POUND CAKE

Makes 1 large tube cake

While taping a cooking show pilot called Moira Sanders' Countryside, I made several of these cakes before and during the shoot. This cake became legendary with the crew and it's no wonder. Doubling the vanilla makes for a cake that's twice as good.

3 cups (750 mL) all-purpose flour

1 tsp (5 mL) baking powder

½ tsp (2.5 mL) fine sea salt

1 cup (250 mL) milk, at room
   temperature

1 Tbsp (15 mL) pure vanilla extract

1 whole vanilla bean, split and seeds
   scraped out

1½ cups (375 mL) butter, at room
   temperature

3 cups (750 mL) granulated sugar

6 large eggs, at room temperature

PREHEAT THE OVEN to 325°F (160°C). Thoroughly butter and flour a 10-inch (25 cm) tube pan with butter. Tap out any excess flour and set the pan aside.

Sift the flour, baking powder and salt into a bowl. Set aside. In a separate small bowl, combine the milk, vanilla extract and seeds from the vanilla bean. Save the vanilla bean pod for another use (see page 88).

Cream the butter at medium speed in the bowl of an electric mixer fitted with the paddle attachment until light and fluffy. Add the sugar slowly, scraping down the sides of the bowl as needed. Beat on high speed for about 3 minutes.

Add 1 egg at a time to the butter mixture. Scrape down the bowl after each addition.

Add the flour and milk mixture, alternating, in 3 parts on the slowest speed, beginning and ending with the flour. Beat until the batter is mixed well.

Scrape the batter into the prepared pan and firmly tap on a counter to allow the batter to settle evenly in the pan. Bake for about 1 hour and 15 minutes, until light golden and a wooden skewer inserted in the centre of the cake comes out clean.

Let the cake cool in the pan for about 30 minutes. Turn the cake out onto a rack. Let the cake cool completely before slicing, if you can wait.

Storage: The cake will keep covered for up to 1 week.

CARAMELIZED PEAR GINGERBREAD CAKE

Serves 8

This cake is almost pudding-like because it's so moist. It took second place at our local Horticultural Society baking contest.

¾ cup (185 mL) butter, divided

1 cup (250 mL) brown sugar, divided

3 medium pears, peeled, cored and quartered

½ cup (125 mL) molasses

½ cup (125 mL) milk

1 cup (250 mL) all-purpose flour

1 tsp (5 mL) ground ginger

1 tsp (5 mL) baking soda

½ tsp (2.5 mL) ground cardamom

½ tsp (2.5 mL) fine sea salt

1 egg, lightly beaten

PREHEAT THE OVEN to 325°F (160°C). Line the bottom of a 9-inch (23 cm) round cake pan with parchment paper and set aside.

Melt ¼ cup (60 mL) butter with ½ cup (125 mL) brown sugar in a small saucepan over medium heat until the mixture is smooth. Spread the mixture over the bottom of the prepared pan.

Place the pear quarters on top of the sugar mixture in 2 lines.

Heat remaining ½ cup (125 mL) butter, remaining ½ cup (125 mL) brown sugar, molasses and milk in a saucepan over medium heat until the mixture becomes smooth. Pour into the bowl of a stand mixer fitted with the paddle attachment.

Sift the flour, ginger, baking soda, cardamom and salt together in a small bowl. Add to the warm molasses mixture. Add the beaten egg and beat until the batter is smooth.

Pour the batter over the prepared pears and spread out evenly.

Bake for 55 minutes, or until a wooden skewer inserted in the centre of the cake comes out clean. Place the cake on a wire rack to cool for about 10 minutes. Place a plate or platter on top of the cake and carefully invert the cake so that the pears are right side up. Serve warm or at room temperature with a dollop of whipped cream.

I have been a member of our local Horticultural Society for several years, hoping that some gardening expertise will rub off on me. At every meeting there is a speaker and I always come away having learned something. Check out gardening clubs in your community and join with a friend.

RASPBERRY CREAM CHEESE BROWNIES

Makes 12 large brownies

These brownies aren't safe anywhere. I sometimes squirrel away large chunks of them in the freezer if I have any left over. But how frustrating when you want just a little nibble and they're all gone. Darn kids...

FOR THE BROWNIES

¾ cup (185 mL) unsalted butter

7 oz (200 g) bittersweet chocolate, chopped

4 large eggs

1½ cups (375 mL) granulated sugar

1 Tbsp (15 mL) pure vanilla extract

1½ cups (375 mL) all-purpose flour

1 tsp (5 mL) baking powder

1 tsp (5 mL) fine sea salt

1 cup (250 mL) fresh or frozen raspberries

2 Tbsp (30 mL) raspberry jam

FOR THE CREAM CHEESE LAYER

8 oz (225 g) cream cheese, at room temperature

½ cup (125 mL) granulated sugar

¼ cup (60 mL) butter, at room temperature

2 eggs

1 tsp (5 mL) pure vanilla extract

FOR THE BROWNIES: Preheat the oven to 325°F (160°C). Line a 9- × 13-inch (23 × 33 cm) baking pan with parchment paper that overhangs the sides of the pan.

Melt the butter and chocolate in a double boiler or a small saucepan set on low heat. Stir constantly until the mixture is smooth. Set aside to cool for 5 minutes.

Beat the eggs and sugar together in the bowl of a stand mixer fitted with the paddle attachment on high for 3 minutes. Add the vanilla and the cooled chocolate mixture. Beat on low speed until combined.

Sift together the flour, baking powder and salt. Add the dry ingredients to the wet ingredients, beating on low speed until combined. Remove about 1½ cups (375 mL) of the batter to a small bowl and set aside. Pour the remaining batter into the pan, spreading evenly. Spread the raspberries evenly over the batter.

Combine the raspberry jam with the reserved batter. Set aside.

Continued . . .

RASPBERRY CREAM CHEESE BROWNIES (*continued*)

FOR THE CREAM CHEESE LAYER: Beat the cream cheese, sugar and butter together in the bowl of a stand mixer fitted with the paddle attachment. Add eggs, one at a time, until thoroughly combined. Add vanilla. Pour the cream cheese mixture over the first layer of brownie batter and raspberries and spread evenly.

Drop the raspberry-jam batter by heaping tablespoons onto the cream cheese layer. Draw lines through the mounds of brownie mixture and cream cheese with a knife until you have a marbleized effect. Bake for 45 minutes or until the brownies appear to be set. The top will be crackled and a toothpick inserted into the centre of the brownies will still be a bit sticky.

Cool the brownies to room temperature on a baking rack. The brownies will be easier to cut if you refrigerate them after they have cooled to room temperature. Cut the brownies into 12 bars, about 3 inches (8 cm) square.

Storage: Refrigerate the brownies in an airtight container for up to 5 days or wrap in a double layer of plastic wrap and freeze for up to 3 months.

PEACH-BLUEBERRY COBBLER

Serves 8

This cobbler recipe, shared by my auntie Carol, is a great example of letting seasonal ingredients be the shining stars at the table. Fruit cobblers are perfect for spur-of-the-moment dinners in the summer. Put it together before dinner, let it bake while you're eating and by the time you've cleared the table you'll have a dessert that showcases the best of summer's bounty. Serve with vanilla ice cream.

6 cups (1.5 L) freshly sliced peaches	1½ cups (375 mL) all-purpose flour
1½ cups (375 mL) fresh blueberries	2 tsp (10 mL) baking powder
1¼ cups (310 mL) granulated sugar, divided	¼ tsp (1 mL) fine sea salt
zest of 1 orange	6 Tbsp (90 mL) butter, chilled
1 tsp (5 mL) pure vanilla extract	1 egg, beaten
	½ cup (125 mL) sour cream

PREHEAT THE OVEN to 400°F (200°C). Butter a 9- × 13-inch (23 × 33 cm) baking pan.

Place the sliced peaches and the blueberries in the prepared pan. Mix ¾ cup (185 mL) sugar, orange zest and vanilla in a small bowl. Sprinkle the sugar mixture over the peaches and blueberries. Place in the oven for 15 minutes.

Meanwhile, combine the flour, remaining ½ cup (125 mL) sugar, baking powder and salt. Mix in the butter using your fingertips until well mixed. In a separate small bowl, combine the egg and sour cream and add to the dry ingredients. Mix gently until the dough comes together.

Remove the peaches and blueberries from the oven and spread the batter over the fruit as evenly as you can. Return to the oven for 30 minutes, or until the dough becomes golden. Serve warm with vanilla ice cream.

Storage: Cobblers don't improve with age. The whole cobbler should be enjoyed the day it's made.

BUBBLE-GUM ICE CREAM

Makes 4 cups (1 L)

People are always asking Gavin and Ellen if they know how lucky they are to have a mom who is such a good cook. When it comes to sweet treats like this, they definitely know!

2 cups (500 mL) whipping cream
2 cups (500 mL) milk
¼ lb (125 g) Double Bubble bubble
   gum (about 10 pieces of gum),
   comic strips reserved for later

6 egg yolks
¾ cup (185 mL) granulated sugar
¼ tsp (1 mL) fine sea salt
¼ cup (60 mL) tiny Chiclets gum,
   optional

PREPARE AN ICE cream maker according to the manufacturer's directions.

Heat the cream and milk in a saucepan set over medium heat, stirring occasionally. Meanwhile, chop the bubble gum into small pieces. Remove the pan from the heat when the cream is steaming but not quite boiling. Add the bubble-gum pieces and allow the mixture to sit for 20–30 minutes.

Whisk together the egg yolks, sugar and salt in a medium-sized bowl until combined.

Strain the cream mixture and discard the bubble-gum pieces. Place the cream back into the saucepan and heat until steaming again. Add a small amount of the hot cream to the beaten egg mixture. Whisk the egg mixture back into the saucepan with the rest of the cream. Cook on low heat, stirring constantly, for 5 minutes or until the custard coats the back of a spoon.

Strain the custard through a fine sieve and chill thoroughly.

Pour the mixture into the ice cream maker. Follow the manufacturer's instructions. If you are using the Chiclets gum, add them to the partially frozen ice cream about half way through the freezing process.

Storage: Freeze in an airtight container for up to 1 week.

VARIATION The bubble gum gives this ice cream a pale pink colour. If you want a brighter pink ice cream, add a smidge of pink food colouring paste to the custard before chilling it in the refrigerator.

(MOIRA) SANDERS HOT FUDGE SAUCE

Makes 2 cups (500 mL)

There used to be an old-fashioned ice cream shop in Detroit, Michigan with the name Sanders. They had the BEST hot fudge sundaes. What made their sauce so good was the combination of caramel and chocolate into one unforgettable sauce. Here's my take on that classic.

1½ cups (375 mL) granulated sugar	½ lb (250 g) milk chocolate, chopped
½ cup (125 mL) water	2 Tbsp (30 mL) butter
1 cup (250 mL) whipping cream	1 tsp (5 mL) pure vanilla extract

COMBINE THE SUGAR and water in a large saucepan. Cook over medium heat until the sugar is dissolved. Brush the insides of the pan with water to get rid of any extra sugar particles. Increase the heat to high when the sugar and water are totally clear. Do not stir. Keep a close eye on the mixture and have the whipping cream beside the stove, ready to go.

Watch for the mixture to turn a dark golden, almost like maple syrup. Turn off the heat and add the whipping cream immediately, being careful, as the caramel will sputter and spit. Stir the mixture and return the pan to low heat to dissolve the caramel.

Remove the caramel from the heat when it is smooth. Add the chocolate, butter and vanilla. Stir until the chocolate is completely dissolved. Serve warm over ice cream.

Storage: Keep leftovers in an airtight container in the refrigerator for up to 3 weeks.

To serve the sauce after it has been in the refrigerator, place the sauce in a heat-proof bowl over a pan of simmering water and warm until it is completely softened and pourable.

This recipe is perfect for banana splits. Serve with Strawberry-Vanilla Freezer Jam (page 234) and chopped cashew nuts or peanuts for an extra special take on this ice cream parlour classic.

WALNUT-SPICE ICEBOX COOKIES

Makes 5 dozen cookies

These cookies are one of my neighbour Nancy's favourites. They're called icebox cookies because they have to spend some time being chilled before baking. The cookie dough is full of holiday spices and chopped walnuts, making them perfect for the Christmas season. When I visit in December, Nancy always serves a plate of these cookies and tea in my favourite cup and saucer.

2¼ cups (560 mL) all-purpose flour

½ tsp (2.5 mL) baking soda

½ tsp (2.5 mL) fine sea salt

1 tsp (5 mL) ground cinnamon

¼ tsp (1 mL) ground nutmeg

¼ tsp (1 mL) ground cloves

1 cup (250 mL) butter

½ cup (125 mL) granulated sugar

½ cup (125 mL) brown sugar

1 egg

2 Tbsp (30 mL) milk

½ cup (125 mL) finely chopped walnuts

30 walnuts, halved, for pressing into the tops of the cookies (approx)

WHISK THE FLOUR, baking soda, salt and spices together in a small bowl. Set aside.

Cream the butter and sugars in the bowl of a stand mixer fitted with the paddle attachment until light. Add the egg and milk and continue beating until combined. Add the flour mixture and stir until combined. Add the finely chopped walnuts to the dough.

Divide the cookie dough in half. Place 1 of these halves of dough on a piece of parchment paper and roll it into a log, about 2 inches (5 cm) in diameter. Repeat with the second half of the dough.

Place the rolls of cookie dough in the refrigerator for at least 2 hours or overnight.

When you are ready to bake the cookies, preheat the oven to 325°F (160°C). Line a baking sheet with parchment paper.

Slice the cookie dough into ½-inch (1 cm) slices. Place the slices on the prepared baking sheet. Press a walnut half onto the top of each cookie.

Bake for 12–14 minutes or until the cookies are golden around the edges. Let the cookies cool on a baking rack.

Storage: Store the cookies in an airtight container for up to 2 weeks.

VARIATION For extra nutty cookies, roll each chilled log of cookie dough in finely chopped walnuts, pressing gently so the nuts stick to the dough. Proceed with cutting the log into cookies and bake according to the recipe.

STAMPED SHORTBREAD COOKIES

Makes 4 dozen cookies

I always feel a strong sense of tradition when I give these cookies away at Christmastime. I collect pretty tins from antique markets and garage sales throughout the year to fill with these cookies during the holidays. My friends in the know make sure they return the tins each December just in time for refills.

2 cups (500 mL) unsalted butter, at
  room temperature
1¼ cups (310 mL) instant-dissolving
  sugar (also known as berry sugar),
  divided

1 cup (250 mL) rice flour
3 cups (750 mL) all-purpose flour

PREHEAT THE OVEN to 300°F (150°C). Line 2 large baking sheets with parchment paper. Set aside.

Cream the butter in the bowl of a stand mixer fitted with the paddle attachment. In a separate medium bowl, combine 1 cup (250 mL) sugar, rice flour and all-purpose flour. Slowly add the dry ingredients to the butter. Mix the dough on medium speed until it begins to come together in a ball.

Scoop walnut-sized balls of cookie dough and roll between your palms until smooth. Place on the prepared pans, leaving at least 2 inches (5 cm) between each ball.

Dip a cookie stamp in a small bowl of the remaining ¼ cup (60 mL) berry sugar. Press the stamp on a ball of cookie dough and press until the dough starts to press beyond the edges of the stamp. Carefully lift the stamp off of the cookie dough. The imprint should be clean and sharp so that it will still be visible once baked. Dip the cookie stamp into the berry sugar again and continue stamping the cookies until they are all imprinted. If you have time, chill the cookies for 15 minutes before baking and the stamp will be clearer on the baked cookie.

Bake for about 30 minutes or until the cookies just barely turn a pale golden colour. Cool for 5 minutes and then place the cookies on a baking rack to cool completely.

Storage: Store the shortbread in an airtight container for up to 2 weeks.

A cookie stamp gives regular shortbread cookies a shot of pizzazz. You can find cookie stamps at specialty kitchen stores or antique shops.

MALTED MILK COOKIES

Makes 3 dozen cookies

This recipe is an old family favourite. These cookies are soft, chewy and suitably malty, a flavour that I especially love in milk shakes. Make a batch of Creamy Iced Coffee (page 266) with the leftover sweetened condensed milk.

FOR THE COOKIES

2½ cups (625 mL) all-purpose flour

¾ cup (185 mL) malted milk powder

½ tsp (2.5 mL) baking soda

¼ tsp (1 mL) fine sea salt

1 cup (250 mL) butter

1 cup (250 mL) granulated sugar

½ cup (125 mL) brown sugar

2 eggs

2 tsp (10 mL) pure vanilla extract

2 Tbsp (30 mL) sweetened condensed milk

FOR THE MALTED MILK FROSTING

½ cup (125 mL) brown sugar

¼ cup (60 mL) butter

¼ cup (60 mL) evaporated milk

½ cup (125 mL) malted milk powder

½ tsp (2.5 mL) pure vanilla extract

2½ cups (625 mL) icing sugar (approx)

FOR THE COOKIES: Preheat the oven to 325°F (160°C). Line a large baking sheet with parchment paper.

Whisk the flour, malted milk powder, baking soda and salt together in a medium bowl.

Cream the butter and sugars together in the bowl of a stand mixer fitted with a paddle attachment until light and fluffy. Add the eggs, one at a time, scraping the bowl down as you go. Add the vanilla and the condensed milk and mix until combined. Add the dry ingredients and mix until thoroughly combined.

Drop rounded tablespoons of cookie dough onto the prepared baking sheets. Bake for 15 minutes, or until the edges start to turn brown. Remove from the oven and cool to room temperature.

FOR THE MALTED MILK FROSTING: Combine the brown sugar, butter and evaporated milk in a saucepan and cook over medium-low heat until the butter is melted. Remove from the heat and add the malted milk powder and vanilla. Whisk in the icing sugar until smooth. Add up to ½ cup (125 mL) more icing sugar until the frosting is a good spreading consistency.

Ice the cookies. Let the cookies sit, uncovered, for at least 30 minutes, or until the icing is set.

Storage: Store in layers of parchment paper in an airtight container for up to 1 week.

APPLE STRUDEL

Makes 3 strudels

Crispy layers of pastry wrapped around apple pie filling is a beautiful thing. I love pulling one of these out of the oven just before a late morning coffee date. This recipe makes three strudels, enough to freeze one or two for another day.

6 large apples, peeled and thinly
  sliced
2 Tbsp (30 mL) fresh lemon juice
¾ cup (185 mL) granulated sugar,
  divided

⅓ cup (80 mL) all-purpose flour
½ tsp (2.5 mL) ground cinnamon
one 1 lb (500 g) package phyllo dough
½ cup (125 mL) melted butter

PREHEAT THE OVEN to 350°F (175°C). Line a baking sheet with parchment paper and set aside.

Toss the sliced apples with lemon juice, ½ cup (125 mL) sugar, flour and cinnamon. Set aside.

Unfold sheets of phyllo and keep covered with a dish towel. Take 1 sheet of phyllo and lay on a flat surface. Brush thoroughly with melted butter. Sprinkle with a pinch of the remaining sugar and place another sheet of phyllo on top. Repeat until 5 sheets have been used, keeping the remaining phyllo covered at all times.

Spread one-third of the apple mixture down the centre of the phyllo sheets, lengthwise. Fold the top over the apples lengthwise, fold in each end and then fold the bottom over. Flip so that the seam of dough is underneath. Place on the prepared baking sheet. Repeat twice more.

Brush tops with melted butter and sprinkle generously with sugar. Cut 3 slits diagonally on the tops of each strudel to vent the steam. Bake for 30 minutes, or until the strudel is golden.

Serve warm or at room temperature.

Storage: These strudels are best eaten the day they are made.

If you are freezing unbaked strudels for later, wrap carefully in 2 layers of plastic wrap and place in a flat area of your freezer or in a shallow plastic container. Don't thaw before baking and add 5–10 minutes to the baking time.

VARIATION Spread 1 cup (250 mL) of your favourite mincemeat on top of the apple mixture and proceed with the recipe.

Special-Occasion Desserts

Orange Birthday Cake   *194*

Chocolate Banana Layer Cake with Banana
   Buttercream   *196*

Violet Cupcakes   *200*

Pumpkin Cheesecake   *203*

White Chocolate Raspberry Yule Log   *204*

Individual Baked Alaskas   *206*

Butterscotch Cream Pie   *208*

Baked Apples   *210*

Caramelized Bread-Crumb Ice Cream   *211*

Steamed Carrot Pudding   *212*

Fortune Cookies   *214*

ORANGE BIRTHDAY CAKE

Serves 10

My grandma made a cake similar to this for my twelfth birthday. She was fearless in the kitchen and I like to think she passed that on to me. It reminds me that it isn't that difficult to create life-long memories for my own kids.

FOR THE CAKES

2¾ cups (685 mL) all-purpose flour

1 Tbsp (15 mL) baking powder

1 tsp (5 mL) fine sea salt

1 cup (250 mL) butter, at room temperature

2 cups (500 mL) granulated sugar

zest of 1 orange

4 eggs, at room temperature

1 tsp (5 mL) pure vanilla extract

1¼ cups (310 mL) orange juice

FOR THE WHIPPED CREAM FILLING

1 Tbsp (15 mL) gelatin

2 Tbsp (30 mL) cold water

2 cups (500 mL) whipping cream

½ cup (125 mL) icing sugar

⅓ cup + ¼ cup (80 + 60 mL) orange juice

FOR THE CHOCOLATE GLAZE

4 oz (120 g) bittersweet chocolate

1½ Tbsp (22.5 mL) butter

FOR THE CAKES: Preheat the oven to 350°F (175°C). Line the bottom of two 9-inch (23 cm) round cake pans with parchment paper. Butter and flour both pans.

Whisk together the flour, baking powder and salt. Set aside.

Cream the butter in the bowl of a stand mixer fitted with the paddle attachment until smooth. Add the sugar and orange zest and beat until fluffy, about 3 minutes. Add the eggs one at a time, beating well after each addition. Add the vanilla and beat until incorporated.

Add the flour mixture to the egg mixture in 3 parts, alternating with the orange juice, beginning and ending with the flour. After each addition, beat until the ingredients are incorporated.

Divide the batter evenly between the prepared pans and smooth the tops. Bake for 30–35 minutes or until a toothpick inserted in the middle comes out clean. Cool the cakes in the pans for about 10 minutes and then remove to a wire rack and cool completely before filling and icing.

FOR THE WHIPPED CREAM FILLING: Sprinkle the gelatin on the 2 Tbsp (30 mL) cold water in a heat-proof ramekin. Let stand 5 minutes. Place the cup into a small pan of boiling water and stir until the gelatin is dissolved. Remove from the heat and set aside.

Whip the cream and the icing sugar in the bowl of a stand mixer fitted with the whisk attachment until it starts to thicken. Continue beating at high speed while you add ⅓ cup (80 mL) orange juice. Slowly add the liquid gelatin until incorporated. Continue beating until stiff. Refrigerate the filling if the cake layers aren't cool yet.

Split each cake in half horizontally, creating 4 thin cake layers. Sprinkle 1 tablespoon (15 mL) of the remaining orange juice on each layer of cake. Place 1 layer on a cake platter.

Divide the whipped cream filling evenly in three parts. Spread one-third of the filling on the first layer of cake, followed by a second layer of cake. Continue layering the filling and cake until there is only the top layer left. Leave the top layer of cake bare.

FOR THE CHOCOLATE GLAZE: Place the chocolate and butter in a heat-proof bowl over a pan of simmering water and stir until melted. Let cool for a few minutes, until slightly thickened. Pour the chocolate on top of the cake and let it drizzle down the sides. Refrigerate for at least 6 hours, but preferably overnight. Let the cake sit at room temperature for at least 30 minutes before serving.

Storage: Keep the cake covered in the refrigerator for up to 3 days.

VARIATION If you want to make the cake without the chocolate glaze, whip 1 cup (250 mL) whipping cream and 1 Tbsp (15 mL) sugar together until thick. Spread over the top of the cake.

CHOCOLATE BANANA LAYER CAKE
WITH BANANA BUTTERCREAM

Serves 10

Layer cakes are one of my favourite ways to serve dessert. They are old-fashioned and not as difficult to put together as one might assume. This is a moist banana chocolate cake iced with the softest banana-flavoured buttercream ever. It's almost as pretty as the birthday girl.

2 cups (500 mL) all-purpose flour

¾ cup (185 mL) cocoa powder

1½ tsp (7.5 mL) baking powder

1 tsp (5 mL) baking soda

¾ tsp (4 mL) fine sea salt

¾ cup (185 mL) butter, at room temperature

1⅔ cups (410 mL) granulated sugar

2 eggs

1 tsp (5 mL) pure vanilla extract

1¼ cups (310 mL) mashed bananas, about 2 large bananas

1 cup (250 mL) buttermilk

1 recipe Banana Buttercream (page 199)

PREHEAT THE OVEN to 350°F (175°C). Line the bottom of two 9-inch (23 cm) round cake pans. Butter and flour both pans and set aside.

Sift the flour, cocoa, baking powder, baking soda and salt together in a medium bowl and set aside. Cream the butter and sugar together in the bowl of a stand mixer fitted with the paddle attachment until the mixture is light and fluffy. Add the eggs one at a time, beating well after each addition. Add the vanilla and beat until incorporated.

In a separate bowl, combine the mashed bananas and buttermilk. Add the dry ingredients to the butter mixture, alternating with the banana mixture, beginning and ending with the flour mixture.

Divide the batter evenly into the prepared pans. Use a digital scale to get the cakes even (about 1½ lb [750 g] in each pan). Smooth the batter and bake for about 35 minutes, or until a toothpick comes out of the cake clean.

Remove the cakes from the oven and let cool for 10 minutes. Remove the cakes from the pans and finish cooling on a cooling rack. If you aren't going to ice the cake right away, wrap the cooled cakes in plastic wrap and keep at room temperature for up to 1 day.

To ice the cake, split each of the cakes in half horizontally (a cake wire does a perfect job but a serrated knife works fine if you have a steady hand). You will have 4 cake layers. Place one of the layers on a cake plate or cake pedestal. Spread about ¾ cup (185 mL) of the buttercream over the first layer. Place the second cake layer on top of the buttercream and continue the layers until you reach the top.

Continued . . .

CHOCOLATE BANANA LAYER CAKE
WITH BANANA BUTTERCREAM (*continued*)

Spread the rest of the buttercream over the top and sides of the cake. If you are going to be serving the cake within a couple of hours, leave the cake at room temperature. If the cake is going to be served much later on or the next day, use toothpicks to carefully cover the cake with a plastic wrap tent. Refrigerate the cake until needed, letting the cake warm up for an hour or so before serving.

Storage: Keep covered in the refrigerator for up to 3 days.

BANANA BUTTERCREAM

Makes 4 cups (1 L)

2 cups (500 mL) milk, divided
1 cup (250 mL) whipping cream
1¼ cups (310 mL) granulated sugar
4 egg yolks
½ cup (125 mL) cornstarch
¼ cup (60 mL) banana liqueur
2 cups (500 mL) butter, at room temperature

HEAT 1 CUP (250 mL) milk and the whipping cream in a medium saucepan over medium heat. In a separate medium bowl, whisk the remaining 1 cup (250 mL) milk with the sugar, egg yolks and cornstarch until smooth. When the milk-cream mixture starts to steam and form bubbles around the edges, slowly add a bit of it to the egg-yolk mixture, whisking constantly. Continue whisking more of the hot milk-cream into the egg mixture until about half of the milk-cream is left. Pour all of the egg mixture back into the saucepan. Whisking constantly, cook over low heat until the mixture has thickened and coats the back of a spoon.

Remove the pan from the heat and quickly pour into a large clean bowl. Whisk the banana liqueur into the custard. Place a piece of parchment paper or plastic wrap on the surface of the custard and let cool until it reaches room temperature, anywhere from 2–3 hours. If you aren't going to make the buttercream at this time, refrigerate the custard. Don't forget to bring the temperature of the custard up to room temperature before proceeding with the recipe.

Cream the butter in the bowl of a stand mixer fitted with the paddle attachment for about 3 minutes, until light and fluffy. With the mixer on medium speed, add the custard to the butter, a spoonful at a time, scraping down the bowl as necessary.

Once all the custard has all been incorporated, scrape the bowl down again and mix for another 30 seconds. The buttercream should be used right away.

Tasting notes from my father-in-law, Max Sanders, after I gave him a piece of this cake to try:

"Moira—The cake was light and not at all overpowering. Nice mild chocolate taste. The icing wasn't too sweet and was also light. The cake and icing together were a nice combination with neither outdoing the other.

This is from a person who is not a real cake lover. An adventure loving cook, I would use this recipe as a base to add some blackberries on top, play with the fillings, but not to blank out the mild chocolate taste or add any sweetness.—Max"

Ladies, he also makes his own pasta from scratch. Call me if you want his phone number!

VIOLET CUPCAKES

Makes 12 cupcakes

Just as the big cupcake craze was starting, I made over 200 of these cupcakes for my friend Annie's wedding (from which I sustained a minor injury forever to be known as "cupcake knee"). Her mom sugared violets from their front yard to top each cupcake. It was truly a match made in heaven.

1½ cups (375 mL) all-purpose flour

1½ tsp (7.5 mL) baking powder

¾ cup (185 mL) granulated sugar

½ cup (125 mL) butter, at room temperature

3 egg whites

1 tsp (5 mL) pure vanilla extract

¾ cup (185 mL) whole milk

½ batch Buttercream (page 199), replacing the banana liqueur with Poire William Eau de Vie or Crème de Violette, if you can find it

violet food colouring, if desired

sugared violet blossoms, for topping (page 202)

PREHEAT THE OVEN to 350°F (175°C). Line a 12-cup muffin pan with paper liners.

Sift the flour and baking powder together in a medium bowl. Set aside.

Cream the sugar and butter together in the bowl of stand mixer fitted with the paddle attachment for 3 minutes. Add the egg whites, one at a time, scraping down the sides as needed. Add the vanilla.

Add the flour mixture to the butter mixture, alternating with the milk, beginning and ending with the flour mixture. Divide the batter evenly in the paper liners. Bake for 18–20 minutes, or until a toothpick inserted into a cupcake comes out clean. Let the cupcakes cool to room temperature.

For the buttercream, prepare the recipe on page 199, replacing the banana liqueur with Poire William or Crème de Violette. Divide the recipe in half and reserve half for another purpose. Gently mix in a dab of violet food colouring, if desired. Continue adding little dabs until you have the colour that you desire. Spread the tops of the cupcakes generously with the violet-coloured buttercream. Top with 1 or more sugared violet blossom.

Storage: Keep the cupcakes in an airtight container for up to 2 days.

These cupcakes are perfectly white as they contain no egg yolks. Use these cupcakes to make Individual Baked Alaskas (page 206).

SUGARED VIOLET BLOSSOMS

Makes 30 blossoms

Violets are only available for a short time each spring and summer and my friend Herbie lets me know when they are at their peak in his garden so I don't miss them. I pick the violets and get straight home and right to work.

30 fresh, perfect-looking unsprayed violet
  blossoms with stem attached
1 egg white
¼ cup (60 mL) extra fine granulated sugar

Place the fresh violet blossoms on the table in front of you. The stems are left on so that you have something to hold the blossoms with.

Whisk the egg white with a fork until it becomes frothy and light. Holding a violet by the stem, gently dip the violet into the frothy egg white, using a small (kid's) paintbrush to moisten all of the nooks and crannies of the flower. Place the blossom in the sugar bowl and gently pour sugar over and around the blossom until it has been completely coated in sugar. Gently pinch the stem off the blossom and place on a baking sheet lined with parchment paper.

Let the blossoms dry for at least 24 hours.

Storage: Keep the blossoms at room temperature in an airtight container for up to 6 months.

PUMPKIN CHEESECAKE

Serves 10

It cannot be overstated: I adore pumpkin pie and anything that resembles pumpkin pie. I've taken some of the best ingredients from my prize winner (see The Harrow Fair Cookbook *for the recipe) and turned them into this family favourite.*

FOR THE CRUMB CRUST

1½ cups (375 mL) graham-cracker crumbs

⅓ cup (80 mL) butter, melted

3 Tbsp (45 mL) granulated sugar

1 tsp (5 mL) ground cinnamon

FOR THE FILLING

1½ lb (750 g) cream cheese, at room temperature

1 cup (250 mL) brown sugar

4 eggs

2 tsp (10 mL) pure vanilla extract

2½ tsp (12.5 mL) ground cinnamon

1 tsp (5 mL) ground mace

2 cups (500 mL) pumpkin purée

1 cup (250 mL) coconut milk

whipped cream, for serving (optional but a very good idea)

PREHEAT THE OVEN to 425°F (220°C). Line the bottom of a 9- or 10-inch (23 or 25 cm) springform pan with parchment paper. Dab the sides of the springform collar with a little soft butter. Cut strips of parchment to fit around the inside of the collar. Set aside.

FOR THE CRUMB CRUST: Combine all of the crust ingredients in a medium bowl. Press the crumb mixture evenly into the springform pan, spreading the crumbs a little ways up the side of the pan. Bake for 5 minutes. Set a timer to make sure you don't forget the crust. Remove from the oven and set aside.

FOR THE FILLING: Beat the cream cheese and brown sugar in the bowl of a stand mixer fitted with the paddle attachment for about 2 minutes. Add the eggs, one at a time, beating well after each. Add the vanilla and spices. Scrape down the sides as you go. Fold in the pumpkin purée and coconut milk with a rubber spatula. Fill the crust with the pumpkin mixture.

Bake for 15 minutes. Lower the heat to 300°F (150°C) and bake approximately 45 minutes more, until set. Turn off the oven and leave the cheesecake inside the oven for an additional 15 minutes. Cool the cheesecake to room temperature and then refrigerate until needed.

Slice the cheesecake with a hot knife. Serve cold or at room temperature with whipped cream.

Storage: Keep the cheesecake, covered, in the refrigerator for up to 5 days.

WHITE CHOCOLATE RASPBERRY YULE LOG

Serves 10

Occasionally I do special catering events for the TV producer that I work for and whenever that situation arises I have a habit of trying new recipes. At a company Christmas party I made two different yule logs as part of the dessert buffet. They were a huge hit, both to look at and to eat, and this is my favourite creation from that evening.

The key to making a yule log look like a log is the method used for creating the chocolate bark. It's ingenious and I wish I could take credit for the idea.

FOR THE WHITE CHOCOLATE BARK
4 oz (120 g) white chocolate, melted

FOR THE LOG

½ cup (125 mL) all-purpose flour

½ tsp (2.5 mL) fine sea salt

6 eggs, separated

1 tsp (5 mL) pure vanilla extract

½ cup (125 mL) granulated sugar

¼ cup (60 mL) icing sugar

FOR THE FILLING

4 egg whites

1 cup (250 mL) granulated sugar

1½ cups (375 mL) butter, at room temperature

1 tsp (5 mL) pure vanilla extract

4 oz (120 g) white chocolate, melted

TO ASSEMBLE

2 Tbsp (30 mL) framboise, or other berry flavoured liqueur

½ cup (125 mL) Two-Burner Raspberry Jam (page 243) or another raspberry jam

FOR THE WHITE CHOCOLATE BARK: Line a large baking sheet with a piece of parchment paper. Spread 4 oz (120 g) melted white chocolate over the parchment paper and spread it thin with an offset spatula. Place a second piece of parchment paper on top of the melted chocolate. Gently roll up the whole thing and place in the refrigerator for at least 2 hours.

FOR THE LOG: Preheat the oven to 350°F (175°C). Line the bottom of an 11- × 17-inch (28 × 42 cm) pan (known as a jelly-roll pan) with parchment paper. Grease the sides of the pan with butter. Set aside.

Whisk together the flour and salt in a small bowl. Set aside.

Place the egg yolks in the bowl of a stand mixer fitted with the whisk attachment and beat on high for 5 minutes. Add the vanilla. Scrape this mixture into a large bowl and set aside.

Wash and dry the mixer bowl and the whisk attachment thoroughly. Whip the 6 egg whites in the clean bowl of the stand mixer fitted with the whisk attachment on high until soft peaks form. Gradually add the granulated sugar and continue beating until stiff peaks form.

Fold half of the egg whites into the egg yolk mixture and stir until combined. Shake the flour mixture over the egg mixture and gently fold together. Add the remaining egg whites and gently stir together until you can't see the egg whites anymore.

Spread the batter evenly in the prepared pan. Bake for about 15 minutes. Cool the cake for 5 minutes. Run a knife around the cake to loosen up the sides. Sprinkle the icing sugar over the cake and lay a clean tea towel on the cake. Cover the cake with a large baking sheet and carefully flip the cake over and remove the jelly-roll pan. Remove the parchment paper and dust the cake with more icing sugar. Roll the cake up, starting at the short end of the cake, leaving some of the tea towel in the roll at the beginning. Let the roll cool to room temperature.

FOR THE FILLING: Whisk the egg whites and sugar in a heat-proof bowl set over a saucepan of simmering water for about 5 minutes. Remove from the heat and place the egg white mixture in the bowl of a stand mixer fitted with the whisk attachment and mix for about 5 minutes or until the mixture is room temperature.

Continue beating the mixture on medium speed and add the butter, a tablespoon at a time. Beat in the vanilla. Set aside about one-third of the mixture to use for the frosting. Melt the white chocolate in a heat-proof bowl set over simmering water. Let the melted chocolate cool for a few minutes and then stir into the frosting that has been set aside.

TO ASSEMBLE: Unroll the cake carefully. Brush the inside of the cake with the framboise liqueur. Spread a thin layer of raspberry jam over the cake and top the jam with the filling mixture. Starting at the short end again, gently roll up the cake and place on a serving plate, seam side down. Spread the white chocolate frosting on the roll without being too neat.

Remove the white chocolate bark from the refrigerator and carefully start to unroll the parchment papers. The chocolate will start to break away in curved pieces, perfect for making bark on the roll. Quickly and carefully arrange the chocolate pieces on the iced roll, making it look like a log with peeling bark. Refrigerate until you are ready to serve.

INDIVIDUAL BAKED ALASKAS

Serves 8

Everyone loves Baked Alaska and it's even more special to be served your own "little Alaska". Baked Alaska is simply a layer of cake and a dome of ice cream, all covered in a glossy meringue and baked in the oven briefly. The trick is having the ice cream portion frozen enough that it doesn't start to melt before the meringue has had a chance to start to turn golden around the swirly edges. With that said, for all of the oohs and ahhs you're going to receive from making this dessert, it's pretty darn simple.

4 cups (1 L) premium ice cream, your choice of flavour, homemade or store-bought

8 un-iced cupcakes (see page 200 for white cupcakes)

5 egg whites

½ cup (125 mL) granulated sugar

¼ tsp (1 mL) cream of tartar

LINE ½-CUP RAMEKINS with plastic wrap, 8 in total. Fill the ramekins with ice cream and smooth it down with the back of a spoon. Fold the plastic wrap over the ice cream and return the ramekins to the freezer for at least a couple of hours, or preferably overnight.

Preheat the oven to 400°F (200°C). Line a large baking sheet with parchment paper.

Slice the tops off of the cupcakes and reserve the tops for another purpose. Remove the paper liner off of each cupcake bottom. Place the cupcake bottoms on the lined baking sheet.

Beat the egg whites in the work bowl of a stand mixer fitted with the whisk attachment for a minute until it starts to get frothy. Add the sugar and the cream of tartar and continue beating until the mixture has thickened and at least doubled in volume. The meringue should be thick and glossy but still spreadable.

Remove the ice cream from the freezer and place each portion on top of a cupcake bottom. Quickly spread the meringue all over each of the ice cream/cupcakes, completely sealing each one so that no holes are showing. Place the baking sheet in the oven for 3 minutes or so, or until the meringue starts to turn golden on the peaks and edges. Remove from the oven, plate individually and serve immediately.

Once homemade ice cream is really frozen, it takes some time to get it to soften up enough to scoop it out into the ramekins. Once you have it in the ramekins, you need to refreeze the ice cream so that it is quite hard when you go to put the Baked Alaskas together. If the homemade ice cream is slightly soft, it will continue to melt at a rapid rate. Store-bought ice cream is a little more accommodating. Use whichever ice cream you feel comfortable with.

BUTTERSCOTCH CREAM PIE

Serves 8

This recipe is dedicated to a woman named Iva Evans from Sharon, Ontario whose butter-scotch pies were the stuff of legends. A lightly whipped cream is just right for topping the pie and I'm a serious fan of the good old graham-cracker crust.

FOR THE CHOCOLATE GRAHAM-CRACKER CRUST

1½ cups (375 mL) graham-cracker crumbs

½ cup (125 mL) butter, melted

2 Tbsp (30 mL) good-quality cocoa powder

2 Tbsp (30 mL) granulated sugar

FOR THE BUTTERSCOTCH FILLING

¼ cup + 2 Tbsp (60 mL + 30 mL) butter

1 cup (250 mL) firmly packed dark brown sugar

3 cups (750 mL) whole milk, divided

⅓ cup (80 mL) cornstarch

4 egg yolks

¼ tsp (1 mL) fine sea salt

1 tsp (5 mL) pure vanilla extract

FOR THE WHIPPED CREAM TOPPING

1½ cups (375 mL) whipping cream

2 Tbsp (30 mL) granulated sugar

½ tsp (2.5 mL) pure vanilla extract

FOR THE CHOCOLATE GRAHAM-CRACKER CRUST: Preheat the oven to 350°F (175°C). Combine all of the crust ingredients in a medium bowl and mix until thoroughly combined. Press the mixture evenly into a 9-inch (23 cm) pie plate. Bake the crust for 10 minutes. Set aside to cool completely.

FOR THE BUTTERSCOTCH FILLING: Melt ¼ cup (60 mL) butter in a medium saucepan. Add the brown sugar and cook over low heat for about 2 minutes, or until the sugar is smooth and bubbly. Remove the pan from the heat and set aside.

Whisk ½ cup (125 mL) milk, cornstarch, eggs and salt together in a large bowl until thoroughly combined. Stir in the remaining milk.

Re-heat the sugar mixture over medium-high heat until the mixture comes to a boil. Reduce the heat to medium-low and carefully pour the milk mixture into the boiling sugar. Stir constantly until the mixture starts to thicken and coats the back of a spoon, about 3–5 more minutes. Remove from the heat and add the remaining 2 Tbsp (30 mL) butter and the vanilla. Place a piece of plastic wrap directly on the surface of the filling and refrigerate for at least 1 hour.

Spoon the filling into the prepared pie shell and smooth the top.

FOR THE WHIPPED CREAM TOPPING: To top the pie using a piping bag and tip, whip the cream, sugar and vanilla in a stand mixer fitted with a whisk attachment. The cream should be whipped until it is stiff, about 1½–2 minutes. Fit a piping bag with a tip of your choice and fill the bag with the whipped cream. Pipe the whipped cream onto the pie.

To top the pie with whipped cream without a piping bag, whip the cream, sugar and vanilla in a stand mixer fitted with a whisk attachment. The cream should be whipped until it is soft, about 1 minute. Spoon the softly whipped cream onto the pie and swirl it around using a spoon or an offset spatula.

Serve immediately or refrigerate until needed.

Storage: This pie is best eaten the day it's made.

BAKED APPLES

Serves 4

I remember making baked apples in a fire pit on a school trip—that's how easy they are to put together. I've embellished my recipe since then and they are perfect when topped with Caramelized Bread-Crumb Ice Cream (page 211) and a drizzle of Butterscotch Sauce (page 213).

4 large Granny Smith apples	2 Tbsp (30 mL) oatmeal
¼ cup (60 mL) firmly packed brown sugar	2 Tbsp (30 mL) currants
	½ tsp (2.5 mL) ground cinnamon
¼ cup (60 mL) butter	1 Tbsp (15 mL) Fresh Bread Crumbs
¼ cup (60 mL) sliced almonds	(page 71)
3 Tbsp (45 mL) finely chopped candied ginger	½ cup (125 mL) apple juice or apple cider

PREHEAT THE OVEN to 375°F (190°C). Core the apples without making any holes in the bottom of the apple. An apple corer may be the easiest way to do this job but you can carefully core an apple with a sharp paring knife as well. Place the apples in a buttered 8-inch (20 cm) baking dish or a medium cast-iron skillet.

Combine all of the remaining ingredients together except for the fresh bread crumbs and the apple cider. Divide the mixture among the 4 apples, filling the cavities of the apples as full as you can. Sprinkle the tops of the apples with a sprinkling of bread crumbs. Pour the apple juice or cider into the baking dish. Cover the baking dish with tin foil.

Bake for 20 minutes and then baste the apples with the juices that have accumulated in the pan. Return the apples to the oven and continue baking for another 20 minutes or until a knife pierces the apple easily all the way through.

Remove the apples from the oven and baste with the juices again. Serve warm or at room temperature with a scoop of Caramelized Bread-Crumb Ice Cream and 1 Tbsp (15 mL) Butterscotch Sauce.

CARAMELIZED BREAD-CRUMB ICE CREAM

Makes 6 cups (1.5 L)

I have several cookbooks from the UK (for a list of my favourites see page 277) and I've come across brown-bread ice cream many times. After trying it once, I was in love. Little caramelized bits of bread crumbs are suspended in a custardy ice cream making this dessert something to write home about.

2 cups (500 mL) Fresh Bread Crumbs (page 71)	8 egg yolks
⅔ cup (160 mL) brown sugar	½ cup (125 mL) granulated sugar
2 cups (500 mL) whipping cream	¼ tsp (1 mL) fine sea salt
2 cups (500 mL) whole milk	1 Tbsp (15 mL) pure vanilla extract

PREPARE AN ICE cream maker according to the manufacturer's directions.

Preheat the oven to 375°F (190°C). Line a large baking sheet with parchment paper.

Toss the bread crumbs and brown sugar in a bowl. Spread the sugared bread crumbs evenly on the lined baking sheet. Bake for 10–12 minutes, or until the crumbs have caramelized into crunchy little clusters. Remove from the oven and let cool to room temperature. Store in an airtight container if you aren't going to be using the crumbs the same day.

Heat the cream and milk in a saucepan set over medium heat, stirring occasionally. In a separate medium bowl, whisk together the egg yolks, sugar and salt until combined. Add a small amount of the hot milk to the beaten egg mixture, stirring constantly. Whisk the egg mixture back into the saucepan with the rest of the milk. Cook on low heat, stirring constantly, for 5 minutes or until the custard coats the back of a spoon.

Strain the custard through a fine sieve into a clean bowl. Place a piece of plastic wrap directly on the surface of the filling and refrigerate for at least 2 hours or preferably overnight.

Pour the custard mixture into the ice cream maker and follow the manufacturer's directions. When the ice cream is partially frozen, add the caramelized bread crumbs and continue churning.

Storage: Freeze in an airtight container for up to 1 week.

RASPBERRY CREAM-CHEESE BROWNIE ICE CREAM Make the Caramelized Bread-Crumb Ice Cream, omitting the bread crumbs and adding 2 cups (500 mL) bite-sized frozen Raspberry Cream-Cheese Brownies (page 179).

STEAMED CARROT PUDDING

Serves 4

This is an old-fashioned steamed pudding recipe handed down from my great-grandmother. The grated potato is an ingredient that you don't see very often in modern desserts but it gives the pudding a moist and distinct texture. I serve this for a traditional holiday dessert, but it would be appreciated on any winter's night, complete with butterscotch sauce (recipe follows).

½ cup (125 mL) butter, softened	½ tsp (2.5 mL) ground cinnamon
1 cup (250 mL) granulated sugar	½ tsp (2.5 mL) ground nutmeg
1 cup (250 mL) all-purpose flour	1 cup (250 mL) grated carrots
1 tsp (5 mL) baking soda	1 cup (250 mL) grated potatoes
½ tsp (2.5 mL) ground cloves	¾ cup (185 mL) dried currants

BRING APPROXIMATELY 3 INCHES (8 cm) of water to a boil in a large stockpot with a tight-fitting lid. Place 4 metal rings from canning jars on the bottom of the pot. Butter a steamed pudding mould with a fitted lid or a ceramic pudding bowl. Set aside.

Cream the butter and sugar for 2 minutes in the bowl of a stand mixer fitted with the paddle attachment until light and fluffy.

Sift together the flour, baking soda, cloves, cinnamon and nutmeg. Add to the butter mixture and blend well. Add the grated carrots, potatoes and currants and mix until incorporated.

Scrape the batter into the prepared pan or bowl. Cover tightly with the lid or 2 layers of buttered aluminum foil. Place the pan or bowl in the stock pot on top of the metal rings so that the water is halfway up the sides of the dishes. Cover the stock pot and steam for about 2 hours, or until firm in the centre. Periodically top up the water so tvhe pot doesn't run dry.

Remove the pudding from the pan and serve warm or at room temperature with Butterscotch Sauce and a scoop of Caramelized Bread-Crumb Ice Cream (page 211).

BUTTERSCOTCH SAUCE

Makes 1½ cups (375 mL)

1 cup (250 mL) firmly packed brown sugar
½ cup (125 mL) butter
½ cup (125 mL) whipping cream
1 Tbsp (15 mL) fresh lemon juice
1 tsp (5 mL) pure vanilla extract

MELT ALL OF the ingredients together in a small saucepan over medium heat. Bring the sauce to a boil. Reduce the heat to medium-low and continue cooking the sauce, stirring frequently until it is slightly thickened, about 5 minutes. Remove the pan from the heat and allow the sauce to cool slightly before serving.

Storage: Keep leftover sauce, covered, in the refrigerator for up to 1 week.

FORTUNE COOKIES

Makes 3 dozen cookies

Fortune cookies are a very special treat that can be made for any sort of occasion. Write the fortunes to match the event (see my lists of fortunes on the following pages or come up with your own) and people will be gob-smacked at your brilliance. These cookies were the first item that my sister made when she started Provisions Food Company in 2012 and they were a big seller. A lucky cookie, perhaps?

4 egg whites	3 Tbsp (45 mL) whipping cream
1 cup (250 mL) ultra-fine sugar	1 tsp (5 mL) pure vanilla extract
1 cup (250 mL) all-purpose flour	pinch fine sea salt
⅓ cup (80 mL) melted butter	

PREHEAT THE OVEN to 375°F (190°C). Line 2 baking sheets with parchment paper and set aside.

Beat the egg whites in the bowl of a stand mixer fitted with the whisk attachment on medium speed until they start to froth up, about 1 minute. Add the sugar and continue whisking for another minute. Add the flour, melted butter, cream, vanilla and salt and whisk until everything is incorporated.

Place about 1 Tbsp (15 mL) batter on the prepared baking sheet for each cookie, leaving each cookie lots of space. Spread the batter in a circle with an offset spatula. Bake only 3 or 4 cookies at a time.

Bake for about 5 minutes or until the cookies have turned golden brown around the edges. Remove the pan from the oven and quickly place a fortune in the centre of each cookie and fold the cookie in half. Bring the 2 corners of the cookie together and press together. Place the folded cookie into a muffin pan to help it keep its shape. Quickly repeat with the remaining cookies.

Continue baking pans of 3 or 4 cookies each time, alternating the baking sheets so that you aren't putting cookie batter on a hot pan.

Storage: Store the cookies in an airtight container for up to 5 days.

Here are some ideas for fortunes from my friends and family. Be inspired to create your own fortunes and sayings for any sort of occasion.

FOOD FORTUNES

EAT YOUR PEAS. · *You're a good egg.* · DON'T PUT ALL OF YOUR EGGS IN ONE BASKET. · *Happiness is egg-shaped.* · IF YOU SEE THE GLASS AS HALF EMPTY, FILL IT UP! · *You are what you eat . . . Beware of sardines.* · GIVE PEAS A CHANCE. · *You're the apple of my eye.* · AND THE BEET GOES ON . . . . *Beware of double-dippers.* · A CUP OF TEA IS THE BEST MEDICINE.

CHRISTMAS FORTUNES

YOU WILL LIVE IN A GINGERBREAD HOUSE WHEN YOU GROW UP. · *Are you on the nice or naughty list?* · ELLEN WANTS A PONY FOR CHRISTMAS. · *Santa prefers single malt scotch.* · GO STAND UNDER THE MISTLETOE. · *Grandma dated Santa before he married Mrs. Claus.* · ONLY 4 SLEEPS 'TIL CHRISTMAS. · *Santa's favourite cookie is chocolate chip.* · YOU WILL EAT LOTS OF TURKEY THIS CHRISTMAS. · *Shortbread should be a food group in December.*

KID'S BIRTHDAY PARTY

BE KIND TO YOUR MOTHER. • *Don't forget to make a big wish.* • WHEN DO ASTRONAUTS EAT? LAUNCH TIME. • *What did the bacon say to the tomato? Lettuce get together.* • WHAT TIME SHOULD YOU GO TO THE DENTIST? TOOTH-HURTY. • *What time are the clowns arriving?* • ALWAYS EAT THE ICING FIRST. • *Pin-the-tail-on-the-Dad is a fun game.* • MAY THE FORCE BE WITH YOU. • *Finicky eaters have to help with dishes.*

VALENTINE'S DAY FORTUNES

YOU ARE THE CRÈME DE LA CRÈME. • *People say chocolate isn't good for you. Clearly they aren't eating enough.* • I HEART YOU. • *Love is the answer.* • THOSE WHO LOVE DEEPLY NEVER GROW OLD. • *You have to give love to get love.* • YOU WILL BE DEEPLY LOVED. • *Elephant shoe.* • I WOULDN'T KICK YOU OUT OF BED FOR EATING CRACKERS. • *Look out for cupid!*

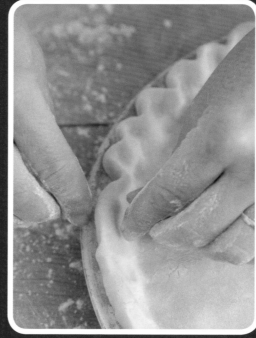

Baking Contest Entries

How to Enter a Baking Contest . . .
and Win!!! *220*

Flaky Pie Dough *222*

Apple-Pear Pie *225*

Sweet Potato Pie *226*

Wild Blueberry Pie *227*

Crabapple Crescent Cookies *228*

Chewy White and Dark Chocolate Chunk
Cookies *229*

HOW TO ENTER A BAKING COMPETITION . . . AND WIN!!!

After years of entering baking contests, I have compiled this list of suggestions that I believe shed some light on the world of baking competitions. It must be said that not all contests share the same sort of rules or have the same level of seriousness. I find that it takes entering once or twice to have a real grasp on the specific contest and on what the judges are looking for.

FOLLOW THE RULES. Read through the prize guide carefully so that you don't miss any of the rules and regulations. Depending on the judges, entries can be disqualified for the smallest of infractions. I once had a seriously perfect piece of apple coffee cake disqualified because I sliced it slightly bigger than the rules demanded (I was trying not to cut into the perfect piece of apple). That half centimetre was the end of that entry.

BE CREATIVE WITH THE THEME. Many fairs have a different theme each year. For example, "Chick It Out" would be a theme all about chicks. The artwork and home crafts will often reflect the theme of that fair. By incorporating the theme into your entry, you are automatically giving yourself a leg up on the competition. An example of incorporating the theme into a baking category might be cutting a piece of pastry out in the shape of a chick and baking it on the top of a double crust pie.

USE TRADITIONAL RECIPES. Judges are looking for the best example of a certain type of baking. If you start adding creative twists, chances are your entry won't be a winner, unless the contest is looking for original creations. If the category is banana bread, the judges are typically looking for the best example of a classic banana bread. A recipe that includes flax seeds and raisins or anything that you wouldn't typically find in a banana bread recipe will usually be passed over.

GO WITH WHAT YOU KNOW. Stick to recipes that you know you can make well. If you want to win (or take second or third place), choose recipes that you are comfortable with. In the introduction for the White Chocolate Raspberry Yule Log (page 204), I mentioned that I like trying new recipes for special events. However, when it comes to entering something in a baking contest, it may help your chances if you go with one of your tried-and-true recipes.

TRY ENTERING LESS POPULAR CATEGORIES. Fewer entries, less competition. It has been my experience that popular categories such as peanut butter cookies or strawberry jam are usually rammed with entries. I look for categories like "best elderberry pie" at the Harrow Fair. First place is $100 and there are usually only a handful of entries every summer. Elderberries aren't available commercially so you have to have a source for the clusters of tiny, sour berries that grow in hedgerows and ditches in some areas of the country. I'm certainly not going to give away the address of my source!

CONSISTENCY COUNTS. For example, if you are entering a jam thumbprint cookie category and they are asking for six cookies, make sure that each cookie is the same size and looks as close to identical as possible. Judges will be looking at the plate as a whole, not only judging the cookies on taste.

GIVE YOURSELF PLENTY OF TIME. When I'm entering a baking contest, generally I want my entries to be as fresh as they can be, especially the pies. However, it's in your best interest to make sure your pies are cooled to room temperature before you drop them off. Some fairs may insist that the pie be placed in a plastic bag (for hygiene reasons) and you can bet that your pie will suffer if it has to cool inside of that plastic bag.

REMEMBER. The most important thing is having fun! Enjoy yourself and don't be a sore loser if you don't win. There's always next year!

FLAKY PIE DOUGH

Makes 5 discs

One day I walked through the door of a small restaurant in Windsor, Ontario and I ended up staying to work for the owner, Elaine, who has become a wonderful friend. At Elaine's, we served lots of desserts and I made batch after batch of pie dough. It was good training and I've tried many pie doughs over the years, but I always return to this old favourite. It has never let me down.

5½ cups (1.38 L) all-purpose flour	1 egg
1 tsp (5 mL) fine sea salt	1 Tbsp (15 mL) white vinegar
1 lb (500 g) good quality lard	1 cup (250 mL) very cold water

COMBINE THE FLOUR and salt in a large bowl. Cut the lard into cubes. Place the lard in the flour. Gently rub the lard into the flour until there are no big chunks left. The mixture should look shaggy.

Whisk the egg and vinegar in a medium bowl. Add 1 cup (250 mL) very cold water to the egg mixture and whisk together. Pour half of the liquid mixture over the flour and gently work the dough together. Add the rest of the liquid to the dough in parts, only adding enough to bring the dough together. You may have a bit of liquid leftover. Continue working gently until the dough comes together in a shaggy lump. Don't overwork the dough.

Divide the dough into 5 discs as evenly as you can. Wrap each disc in plastic wrap and refrigerate for at least 1 hour.

Storage: Keep in the refrigerator for up to 1 week.

To make it easier to roll out dough that has been refrigerated for a while, let the dough warm up on the counter for 15–30 minutes before you need to use it.

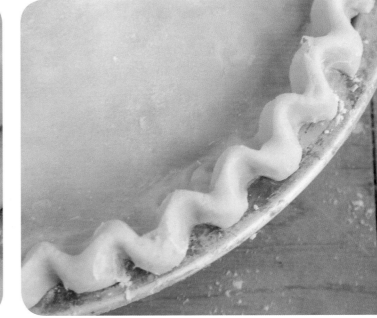

APPLE PIE FOLLY Evie, our summertime neighbour, makes a mean apple pie. Years before I ever thought of entering my baking at the Harrow Fair, her daughter's boyfriend talked her into entering an apple pie. He even offered to enter it for her. She put her heart and soul into making that pie and handed it over to the boyfriend. That was the last anyone ever heard of that pie. We know now that the pie never made it to the fairgrounds that summer's day. And that was the end of the boyfriend, too.

APPLE-PEAR PIE

Serves 8

One of the most exciting things about the Harrow Fair for me is the pie auction. In 2013, this pie was auctioned off for $1125.00. Not a record-breaking amount, but still a huge thrill for me!

I would love to see more fairs take inspiration from the Harrow Fair in the way they run their baking contests. All ribbon-winning pies are sent off (with the baker's permission) to the main stage for auction, shortly after they have been judged. The auction attracts all sorts of people, including local politicians and business owners with deep pockets, and over 100 pies are auctioned off. The proceeds, which total more than $10,000 every year, are donated to a local children's organization, the pies aren't left sitting around all weekend, and there is a thriving competition between bakers. A win-win situation for everyone.

4 cups (1 L) peeled, cored and thinly sliced ripe Bosc pears	1 tsp (5 mL) ground cinnamon
4 cups (1 L) peeled, cored and thinly sliced Golden Delicious apples	½ tsp (2.5 mL) fine sea salt
¾ cup (185 mL) granulated sugar, plus more for sprinkling	¼ tsp (1 mL) ground nutmeg
	2 Tbsp (30 mL) butter
	2 discs Flaky Pie Dough (page 222)
2½ Tbsp (37.5 mL) cornstarch	1 egg
	1 Tbsp (15 mL) milk

PREHEAT THE OVEN to 450°F (230°C).

Combine the sliced pears and apples with the sugar, cornstarch, cinnamon, salt and nutmeg in a large bowl and toss until the fruit is thoroughly coated.

Roll out 1 disc of the pie dough and fit it into a 9-inch (23 cm) deep-dish pie plate. Place the fruit mixture in the pie shell and arrange in a heaping mound. Place dabs of butter on the pears.

Roll out the other disc of pie dough and apply the dough over the pears. Trim the excess pie dough from the edges and crimp the edges together.

Whisk the egg and milk together and brush over the top of the pastry. Sprinkle with granulated sugar. Cut slits in the top crust to allow the steam to escape, creating a design of your choice.

Bake the pie for 10 minutes. Reduce the oven temperature to 350°F (175°C) and continue baking for about 40 minutes, or until the crust is golden brown and the filling is bubbling. You may wish to place a drip catcher under the pie, preferably on the lower rack.

Allow the pie to cool to room temperature before serving.

Storage: This pie can be covered with aluminum foil and stored at room temperature for up to 2 days.

SWEET POTATO PIE

Serves 8

When entering baking contests, visual appeal is way more than half the battle. As with any food, if it looks good, we are much more inclined to enjoy it, or at least to want to try it. Some judges may not even taste an entry if it isn't visually appealing. In the case of the sweet potato pie, boiling the sweet potatoes makes for a bright orange filling and is just plain "prettier. If you aren't making this to enter in a contest, serve with lots of whipped cream.

1 disc Flaky Pie Dough (page 222)

¾ cup (185 mL) firmly packed brown sugar

1 tsp (5 mL) ground cinnamon

½ tsp (2.5 mL) fine sea salt

½ tsp (2.5 mL) ground ginger

¼ tsp (1 mL) ground nutmeg

2 eggs

2½ cups (625 mL) cooked and mashed sweet potatoes

1 cup (250 mL) whipping cream

PREHEAT THE OVEN to 450°F (230°C).

Roll out the disc of pie dough and fit it into a 9-inch (23 cm) pie plate. Trim the excess pie dough and crimp the edges.

Mix the brown sugar, cinnamon, salt, ginger and nutmeg thoroughly in a large bowl. Whisk in the eggs. Add the mashed sweet potato, making sure that the mixture is well blended. Stir in the whipping cream. Pour into the prepared pastry shell.

Bake for 20 minutes, then reduce the heat to 350°F (175°C) and continue baking 30 minutes longer, or until the filling is slightly firm and the crust is golden brown. Cool to room temperature and serve.

Storage: This pie can be covered in plastic wrap and stored in the refrigerator for up to 2 days.

WILD BLUEBERRY PIE

Serves 8

This pie won first prize at the Harrow Fair where I used a combination of wild blueberries and cultivated blueberries. My dad, not always known as the family baker, has become a blueberry pie-making expert and has even won a ribbon in the Men's Only category at the fair. Thank you to my dad for sharing his recipe.

5 cups (1.25 L) wild blueberries, domestic blueberries or a combination of both (fresh or frozen)	¼ cup (60 mL) cornstarch
	pinch fine sea salt
	2 discs Flaky Pie Dough (page 222)
	1 egg
½ cup (125 mL) water	1 Tbsp (15 mL) milk
2 Tbsp (30 mL) fresh lemon juice	1 tsp (5 mL) granulated sugar
¾ cup (185 mL) granulated sugar	

COMBINE THE BLUEBERRIES, water and lemon juice in a large saucepan over medium heat. When the blueberries start to break down, add the sugar, cornstarch and salt. Stir constantly until the mixture becomes thick. Remove from the heat and cool completely.

Preheat the oven to 400°F (200°C).

Roll out 1 disc of the pie dough and line a 9-inch (23 cm) pie plate. Spread the blueberry mixture in the pie shell evenly.

Roll out the other disc of pie dough and place the dough over the blueberry filling. Trim the excess pie dough from the edges and crimp the edges together.

Whisk the egg and milk together and brush over the top of the pastry. Sprinkle with granulated sugar. Cut slits in the top crust to allow the steam to escape, creating a design of your choice.

Bake the pie for about 45 minutes, or until the crust becomes golden brown and the blueberry mixture starts to bubble up. You may wish to place a drip catcher under the pie, preferably on the lower rack.

Cool to room temperature and serve with a dollop of vanilla ice cream.

Storage: This pie can be covered with aluminum foil and stored at room temperature for up to 2 days.

WILD BLUEBERRIES are available at the end of the summer in markets and grocery stores. Wild blueberries are tiny and packed with flavour. If you've ever picked them yourself, you'll know why they are so expensive.

CRABAPPLE CRESCENT COOKIES

Makes 4 dozen cookies

I credit these little cookies for sealing the deal with my publisher Whitecap Books for The Harrow Fair Cookbook. *When my sister and I met with the publisher to talk over our ideas for the book, I whipped up a batch of these cookies to help sweeten the pot.*

FOR THE COOKIE DOUGH

1 cup (250 mL) butter, at room temperature

8 oz (225 g) cream cheese, at room temperature

¼ cup (60 mL) granulated sugar

1 tsp (5 mL) pure vanilla extract

¼ tsp (1 mL) fine sea salt

2 cup (500 mL) all-purpose flour

FOR THE FILLING

¾ cup (185 mL) dried currants

6 Tbsp (90 mL) granulated sugar

¼ cup (60 mL) brown sugar, packed

½ tsp (2.5 mL) ground cinnamon

FOR THE COOKIES

½ cup (125 mL) Crabapple Jelly (page 240), or your favourite jam or jelly

1 egg, beaten

2 Tbsp (30 mL) milk

3 Tbsp (45 mL) granulated sugar

FOR THE COOKIE DOUGH: Cream the butter and cream cheese together in the bowl of a stand mixer with the paddle attachment until light. Add the sugar, vanilla and salt and mix until combined. With the mixer on low speed, add the flour and mix until the dough comes together. Divide the dough up into 4 equal pieces and form each one into a disc. Wrap each one in plastic wrap and refrigerate for 1 hour.

FOR THE FILLING: Combine the currants, granulated sugar, brown sugar and cinnamon in a medium bowl and set aside until needed.

FOR THE COOKIES: Preheat the oven to 350°F (175°C).

Roll each disc of dough into a 9-inch (23 cm) circle on a well-floured board. Spread the dough with 2 Tbsp (30 mL) of crabapple jelly and sprinkle with ½ cup (125 mL) of filling. Press the filling lightly into the dough. Cut the circle into 12 equal wedges. Starting with the outside wide edge, roll up each wedge. Place the cookies, points tucked under, on a baking sheet lined with parchment paper.

Whisk the egg and milk together in a small bowl. Brush each cookie with the egg wash. Sprinkle each cookie with sugar. Bake for 15–18 minutes, until lightly browned. Remove to a wire rack and let cool.

Storage: Store the cookies in an airtight container for up to 5 days.

CHEWY WHITE AND DARK CHOCOLATE CHUNK COOKIES

Makes 2 dozen cookies

Everything that I have tried out of the Sugar *cookbook by Anna Olson has been a winner, including her chocolate chip cookies. The secret to Anna's cookies is the cornstarch; just a little bit of cornstarch creates a chewiness that doesn't go away. I've added a combination of bittersweet and white chocolate making these cookies a real family favourite.*

¾ cup (185 mL) butter

1 cup (250 mL) firmly packed brown sugar

¼ cup (60 mL) granulated sugar

1 egg

2 tsp (10 mL) pure vanilla extract

2 cups (500 mL) all-purpose flour

2 tsp (10 mL) cornstarch

1 tsp (5 mL) baking soda

½ tsp (2.5 mL) fine sea salt

½ cup (125 mL) chopped bittersweet chocolate

½ cup (125 mL) chopped white chocolate

PREHEAT THE OVEN to 350°F (175°C). Line a baking sheet with parchment paper.

Cream together the butter and sugars in the bowl of a stand mixer fitted with the paddle attachment. Add the egg and vanilla and mix for 1 minute on medium speed.

In a separate medium-sized bowl, sift together the flour, cornstarch, baking soda and salt. Slowly add the dry ingredients to the wet ingredients until combined and the dough comes together in a ball. Add the chopped white and dark chocolate and mix until combined.

Form the cookies by rolling about 2 Tbsp (30 mL) of cookie dough together in a ball. Place each ball on the baking sheet and press it down gently with your palm. Don't over crowd the cookie sheet.

Bake for 10 minutes or until the cookies turn golden and the smell starts to drive your family crazy.

Transfer the cookies to a baking rack to cool.

Storage: Store the cookies in an airtight container for up to 5 days.

Pantry and Preserves

Preserves and Pantry Items   *232*
Strawberry-Vanilla Freezer Jam   *234*
Red and Black Jam   *237*
Black and Blue Jam   *238*
Peach Freezer Jam   *239*
Crabapple Jelly   *240*
Two-Burner Raspberry Jam   *243*
Pear-Cranberry Chutney   *244*
Homemade Pizza Sauce   *246*
All-Season Tomato Sauce   *247*
Chili Sauce with Fruit   *248*
Pickled Green Beans   *249*
Homemade Mayonnaise   *250*
Chicken Stock   *251*
Veggie Stock   *252*

PRESERVES AND PANTRY ITEMS

There are two ways of preserving foods in this book.

- One is the method of cooking the produce with salt or sugar according to the recipe, filling the sterilized jars and then processing in a boiling water canner. These preserves are then shelf stable for a year or more.

- The second is freezing. I often freeze tomato sauce and pizza sauce rather than going through the process of traditional canning. And the same goes for my freezer jams. Foods that are preserved by freezing are not meant to be kept at room temperature after they have been thawed. They usually have a fresher taste and it isn't necessary to use sterilized jars or to be processed in a boiling water canner.

As you read through the recipes in this section, you'll see that each method has its pros and cons, depending on what your situation is or what you want your end result to be. I like having the option of using both methods.

Here's the equipment you'll need to get started:
- Jars
- Rings
- Tops
- Canning Set
- Boiling Water Canner

JARS Always use specially made canning jars. Canning jars can be used over and over again and they are available at most hardware and grocery stores. I think the perfect size for canning jams and condiments is the 1 cup (250 mL) size and the perfect size for pickling and canning whole fruits is either the 2 cups (500 mL) or 4 cups (1 L) size.

To prepare the jars, place them in the boiling water canner and bring to a boil. Reduce the heat to a simmer and keep the jars in the canner until ready to fill. Alternatively, I sometimes run a load of jars through the dishwasher without detergent. Once the cycle is finished, place the jars on a baking sheet in a 250°F (120°C) oven until you are ready to fill them.

RINGS The metal rings that are made to use on canning jars can also be reused as long as they aren't bent while being opened. I keep a bag of metal rings and new tops in my canning cupboard so that I'm always ready.

TOPS The snap tops for canning jars are the only part of the canning system that can't be reused (recycle if your area allows). The tops have a rubber seal around the edge that helps to seal the top to the jar when heated.

To sterilize the rings and tops, place them in a medium saucepan full of water and bring to a boil. Reduce the heat to low and keep them hot until you are ready to seal the jars. They can also be sterilized in the boiling water canner but make sure you can fish them out when you need them.

CANNING SET This can be found at most hardware stores or places that sell canning jars. The set contains a wide-mouth funnel, a jar lifter and a small wand with a magnetic end. The wide-mouth funnel keeps drips and spills to a minimum when you are filling the jars. The jar lifter is a must for grabbing hot jars safely. The wand with the magnet is the perfect tool for picking lids and tops out of boiling water. These sets are usually inexpensive and are essential for a home canner.

BOILING WATER CANNER A large pot (usually aluminum) fitted with a metal rack insert, these are usually available at local hardware and grocery stores. Fill the pot at least half full and bring to a boil while you start your canning. Place the filled and sealed jars in the metal rack, making sure the jars are completely covered by water. Bring the water to a hard boil and then start the timer for the number of minutes indicated in the recipe. When the processing is finished, use a jar lifter and carefully remove the jars from the boiling water. Place the jars on the counter to cool and enjoy the sweet sound of success as the lids *pop*, proving that jar is officially sealed.

STRAWBERRY-VANILLA FREEZER JAM

Makes five 8 oz (240 mL) jars

I was recently granted permission to observe the baked good and canning judging at the Harrow Fair. I was lucky to sit in on the judging of the jams and jellies done by a retired canning expert from the Harrow Experimental Farm and he really knew his stuff. In order to win, freezer jams have to be very bright in colour and taste just like fresh fruit.

8 cups (2 L) sliced fresh strawberries

2½ cups (625 mL) sugar with
 pectin added

2 Tbsp (30 mL) fresh lemon juice

1 vanilla bean, split and the seeds
 scraped out for another use
 (try Vanilla Bean Tapioca Pudding,
 page 88)

ASSEMBLE 5 CLEAN 8 oz (250 mL) jars, lids and rings.

Place all of the ingredients in a large stockpot. Bring to a boil over medium-high heat, stirring often. Remove from the heat.

Skim off any foam that rises to the surface of the jam. Remove the vanilla bean and ladle the jam into the clean jars. Top with the lids and rings and leave to cool to room temperature.

Storage: This jam will keep in the refrigerator for up to 1 month or it can be frozen for up to 1 year.

FREEZER JAM

- Fresh fruit flavour
- More kid-friendly to make than the traditional jams
- Needs pectin
- Requires clean jars but they don't have to be sterilized
- No processing in the boiling water canner
- Can be stored in the freezer for several months or in the refrigerator for a few weeks.

RED AND BLACK JAM

Makes four 8 oz (250 mL) jars

Once you are comfortable with the basics of jam making, you can mix and match all sorts of different fruits and berries.

3½ cups (875 mL) red raspberries

2½ cups (625 mL) black raspberries
or blackberries

2 cups (500 mL) granulated sugar

3 Tbsp (45 mL) fresh lemon juice

PREPARE FOUR 8 OZ (250 mL) jars, lids and rings for canning, keeping them in the boiling water canner while you make the jam.

Stir the raspberries, black raspberries (or blackberries), sugar and lemon juice together in a large stockpot. Let the mixture sit at room temperature for 1 hour until the sugar is mostly dissolved, stirring occasionally.

Bring the mixture to a boil over medium-high heat, stirring often. Simmer the jam over medium heat, continuing to stir often, for 20 minutes or until the jam thickens and runs off the side of a spoon in heavy drops. Remove from the heat. Skim off any foam that rises to the surface of the jam.

Fill and seal the hot jars 1 at a time, according to the manufacturer's directions. Place the jars in the boiling water canner and process for 10 minutes. Remove the jars from the canner and let cool.

Storage: Enjoy at any point, but use within 1 year.

TRADITIONAL JAMS
- Rich fruit flavour
- Don't need pectin
- Keep for months at room temperature
- Require sterilized jars
- Finished jars have to process in the boiling water canner

BLACK AND BLUE JAM

Makes four 8 oz (250 mL) jars

One summer I was making a batch of jam at my parents' house and my mom was watching over my shoulder. "You're stirring too hard," she told me.

I handed her the spoon and she proceeded to show me how she cooks her jams. Mom uses a maslin pan and a straight-sided spoon. As she's stirring, she very gently gets the jam moving in the pot without creating a splash up the inside of the pan. Mom is meticulous when it comes to canning and preserving.

At that moment I realized that my mom is like a Zen master in the art of preserving. Jam making is, in fact, a simple process—but as always, the love is in the details.

3 cups (750 mL) blackberries	3 Tbsp (45 mL) fresh lemon juice
3 cups (750 mL) blueberries	2 cups (500 mL) granulated sugar

PREPARE FOUR 8 OZ (250 mL) jars, lids and rings for canning.

Place the blackberries, blueberries and lemon juice in a large stockpot. Add the sugar. Let the mixture sit at room temperature for 1 hour until the sugar is mostly dissolved, stirring occasionally.

Bring the mixture to a boil over medium-high heat, stirring often. Simmer the jam over medium heat, continuing to stir often, for 20 minutes or until the jam thickens and runs off the side of a spoon in heavy drops. Remove from the heat. Skim off any foam that rises to the surface of the jam.

Fill and seal the hot jars 1 at a time, according to the manufacturer's directions. Process the jars in the boiling water canner for 10 minutes. Remove the jars from the canner and let cool.

Storage: Enjoy at any point, but use within 1 year.

MASLIN PANS are very solid and heavy and are made specifically for making jams and preserves. The top of the pan is larger than the bottom, leaving less space for the jam to scorch on the bottom and more space for the water to evaporate from the surface. It's the perfect jam pot, but can be used for a wide variety of other jobs in the kitchen.

PEACH FREEZER JAM

Makes five 8 oz (250 mL) jars

Freezer jams taste so fresh, and pulling a jar of this jam out of the freezer in the middle of winter feels like a gift of summer. Try this jam in the recipe for Roasted Peameal Bacon (page 36).

8 cups (2 L) fresh peach slices

2½ cups (625 mL) sugar with pectin added

2 Tbsp (30 mL) fresh lemon juice

ASSEMBLE 5 CLEAN 8 oz (250 mL) jars, lids and rings.

Place all of the ingredients in a large stockpot. Bring to a boil over medium-high heat, stirring often. Remove from the heat.

Skim off any foam that rises to the surface of the jam. Ladle the jam into the clean jars. Top with the lids and rings and leave to cool to room temperature.

Storage: This jam will keep in the refrigerator for up to 1 month or it can be frozen for up to 1 year.

CRABAPPLE JELLY

Makes about ten 8 oz (250 mL) jars

Crabapples make my favourite jelly. At its best, the jelly is a crystal clear pink jewel colour. The flavour is subtle but recognizably apple-ish.

4 quarts (4 L) fresh ripe crabapples, approximately 4 lb (2 kg)

6 cups (1.5 L) water

2 Tbsp (30 mL) fresh lemon juice

one 85 mL package liquid pectin

9 cups (2.25 L) granulated sugar

REMOVE THE BLOSSOM and stem ends from the apples. Cut the apples in halves or quarters and place in a large stockpot. Add the water and bring to a boil. Simmer, covered, for 10 minutes.

Line a colander or strainer with 4 layers of cheesecloth (or you can use a jelly bag) and place the colander over a large bowl. Place the crabapple mixture in the colander and allow the juice to drip through on its own. Do not squeeze the crabapple pulp. Leave to drip for 2–3 hours or overnight.

Prepare ten 8 oz (250 mL) jars, lids and rings for canning. Hold the sterilized jars in the boiling water canner until needed.

Place 7 cups (1.75 L) crabapple juice in a clean stockpot. If you don't have enough juice, you can add up to ½ cup (125 mL) water. Add the lemon juice and liquid pectin. Bring to a boil over high heat. Add the sugar.

Return to a boil and boil hard for 1 minute. Remove from the heat. Stir and skim the top for 5 minutes.

Fill and seal the hot jars one at a time. Process the jars in the boiling water canner for 10 minutes. Let the jelly sit on the counter for 24 hours before moving to the pantry.

Storage: Enjoy at any point, but use within 1 year.

CRABAPPLES can be found at farmers' markets, specialty orchards or, if you're lucky, in your neighbour's backyard. There are different varieties of crabapples with different characteristics. One of my favourites is the Pink Beauty, which have red skins and pink flesh. I get all of my crabapples from Siloam Orchards, an apple-lover's delight that sells the largest variety of heirloom apple trees in Canada.

TWO-BURNER RASPBERRY JAM

Makes three 8 oz (250 mL) jars

While reading a cookbook on our sailboat one summer's day, I started thinking about making jam on the boat. That sparked the idea for "two-burner jam." With just two burners, two large pots, jars and tops and your ingredients, you can preserve just about anything. Since then, I've canned jams and chutneys in front of audiences with nothing more than an extension cord and the supplies I just mentioned. I made my Two-Burner Raspberry Jam while we were docked at Aubrey Island in the Thousand Islands.

5½ cups (1.38 L) fresh or frozen
raspberries

2 Tbsp (30 mL) fresh lemon juice
2 cups (500 mL) granulated sugar

BRING A LARGE stockpot of water to a boil. Reduce the heat to medium to keep the water simmering. Place three 8 oz (250 mL) jars, lids and rings in the simmering water until needed.

Place the raspberries and lemon juice in a second large stockpot. Add the sugar. Bring the mixture to a boil over medium-high heat, stirring often. Simmer the jam over medium heat, continuing to stir often, for 20 minutes or until the jam thickens and runs off the side of a spoon in heavy drops. Remove from the heat. Skim off any foam that rises to the surface of the jam.

Fill and seal the hot jars one at a time. Place the sealed jars in the stockpot of hot water. Bring the water back to a boil and continue boiling for 10 minutes. Remove the jars from the water and let cool.

Storage: Enjoy at any point, but use within 1 year.

PEAR-CRANBERRY CHUTNEY

Makes four 8 oz (250 mL) jars

A no-brainer for serving with roast chicken, turkey or even a sharp cheddar cheese, little jars of this chutney make thoughtful holiday gifts. This is a multi-ribbon winner and one of the recipes I make for my two-burner demonstrations (page 243).

4 large ripe pears

3 cups (750 mL) fresh or frozen
   cranberries

1 cup (250 mL) diced yellow onion

¾ cup (185 mL) firmly packed brown
   sugar

¾ cup (185 mL) apple cider vinegar

zest and juice of 3 clementines

1 tsp (5 mL) fine sea salt

1 cinnamon stick

10 allspice berries

PREPARE FOUR 8 oz (250 mL) or eight 4 oz (120 mL) jars, tops and rings for canning.

Peel the pears and chop into small pieces. Place in a large pot along with all the other ingredients.

Bring to a boil, then reduce the heat and simmer for 30 minutes or until thickened.

Take the time to remove the cinnamon stick and all of the allspice berries.

Fill and seal the hot jars one at a time. Process the jars in a boiling water canner for 10 minutes.

Storage: Enjoy at any point, but use within 6 months.

HOMEMADE PIZZA SAUCE

Makes nine 8 oz (250 mL) jars

Homemade Pizza (page 148) is one of my favourite things to make when we are having families over for a meal. People are always blown away by the taste of the pizza sauce and I always have a stash of it in my freezer or cupboard to use at a moments notice. Chances are you already have most of the ingredients for this sauce in your refrigerator or pantry and if you're anything like me, you'll never get tired of reaching for ingredients that you've made yourself.

⅓ cup (80do mL) olive oil

2 cups (500 mL) chopped onions

one 12 oz (375 mL) jar roasted red peppers, drained

½ cup (125 mL) chopped sun-dried tomatoes (oil packed)

½ cup (125 mL) Kalamata olives

¼ cup (60 mL) minced garlic

three 28 oz (796 mL) cans whole tomatoes, with juice

¼ cup (60 mL) chopped fresh basil (or 2 tsp [10 mL] dried basil)

1 Tbsp (15 mL) dried oregano

2 tsp (10 mL) fine sea salt

1 tsp (5 mL) freshly ground black pepper

1 tsp (5 mL) granulated sugar

½ tsp (2.5 mL) dried red chili flakes

½ tsp (2.5 mL) anchovy paste

HEAT THE OIL in a large stockpot over medium heat and add the chopped onions. Cook the onions for about 10 minutes, until they are very soft.

Add the roasted red peppers, sun-dried tomatoes, olives and garlic. Continue cooking for another 10 minutes or so, stirring well.

Add the rest of the ingredients and bring to a boil, breaking up the tomatoes with a wooden spoon as it cooks. Reduce the heat to a simmer and continue to cook the sauce for about 2 hours, stirring occasionally, or until the sauce is thick.

Purée the sauce using an immersion blender or a food processor.

Fill and seal the jars one at a time. Process the jars in a boiling water canner for 10 minutes.

Storage: Enjoy at any point, but use within 1 year.

Instead of canning the sauce, freeze in 1 cup (250 mL) portions for up to 6 months.

ALL-SEASON TOMATO SAUCE

Makes 3 cups (750 mL)

Here is an easy way to make an all-purpose tomato sauce that is suited to most recipe needs. The key is to use the best-quality store-bought canned tomatoes that you can find. San Marzano tomatoes, an Italian variety, are now widely available. I keep containers of this recipe in the freezer for those meals that sort of creep up on you. Use this tomato sauce in Cabbage Rolls (page 154) and Stuffed Shells (page 169).

one 28 oz (796 mL) can whole or diced San Marzano tomatoes	4 basil leaves
½ cup (125 mL) finely chopped onion	½ tsp (2.5 mL) fine sea salt
2 Tbsp (30 mL) butter	¼ tsp (1 mL) freshly ground black pepper

COMBINE THE TOMATOES and their juices with the rest of the ingredients in a large saucepan. Bring to a boil, reduce the heat and simmer for about 30 minutes. Break any whole tomatoes up with a spoon while the sauce is simmering.

For a chunky sauce, serve as is. For a smooth sauce, pulse the sauce in a food processor until mostly smooth or purée with an immersion blender.

Storage: Serve immediately or refrigerate, covered, for up to 5 days. Freeze any or all of the sauce in airtight containers for up to 6 months.

CHILI SAUCE WITH FRUIT

Makes five 16 oz (500 mL) jars

This is my friend Frances' prize-winning recipe for chili sauce. There is nothing hot and spicy about this chili sauce. It's a pleasing combination of sweet and savoury flavours and it goes extremely well with Meatloaf (page 129), Cottage Pie (page 130), Winter Meat Pies (page 156) and any roasted meats.

6 cups (1.5 mL) chopped, peeled and seeded fresh tomatoes

4 cups (1 L) chopped onions

4 cups (1 L) peeled and chopped apples

3 cups (750 mL) peeled and chopped pears

3 cups (750 mL) finely chopped celery

3 cups (750 mL) finely chopped sweet red peppers

2 cups (500 mL) finely chopped sweet green peppers

1½ cups (375 mL) granulated sugar

1 Tbsp (15 mL) fine sea salt

¾ cup (185 mL) white vinegar

1½ Tbsp (22.5 mL) pickling spices, wrapped in a square of cheesecloth and tied with string

PLACE ALL OF the ingredients in a large stockpot. Bring to a boil. Reduce the heat to low and simmer for about 4 hours, stirring frequently.

Prepare five 16 oz (500 mL) jars, lids and rings. Before canning, bring the chili sauce back to a boil. Fill the jars according to the manufacturer's directions. Process the jars in the boiling water canner for 20 minutes.

Storage: Enjoy at any point, but use within 1 year.

SLOW-COOKER CHILI SAUCE Place all of the ingredients into a large slow cooker (I use a 6 quart (6 L) slow cooker) and cook on high for about 14 hours, stirring once in a while. After 6 hours, place a wooden spoon in the pot to crack the lid. Remove the lid after 12 hours and keep cooking on high to reduce the liquid.

Prepare 5 jars, lids and rings. Before canning, bring the chili sauce back to a boil. Fill the jars according to the manufacturer's directions. Process the jars in a boiling water canner for 20 minutes.

PICKLING SPICE is a premade blend of herbs and spices. It is generally a combination of mustard seeds, coriander seeds, bay leaves, allspice, cloves, cinnamon bark, dried red chili flakes, cardamom, black pepper and mace. Your local bulk food store is a good place to purchase pickling spice.

· ·

PICKLED GREEN BEANS

Makes five 16 oz (500 ml) jars

Yes, another ribbon winner. These beans are zingy and crunchy. Serve with Grilled Pimento-Cheese Sandwiches (page 72).

3 cups (750 mL) pickling vinegar	5 large garlic cloves, peeled
3 cups (750 mL) water	2 lb (1 kg) fresh green beans, topped
3 Tbsp (45 mL) pickling salt	and cut into 3–4-inch (8–10 cm)
5 large fresh dill heads	pieces

PREPARE FIVE **16** oz (500 ml) jars, lids and rings for canning. Hold the sterilized jars in the boiling water canner until needed.

Bring the pickling vinegar, water and pickling salt to a boil in a large stockpot. Continue to simmer the brine over medium heat.

Fill one jar at a time with 1 dill head, 1 garlic clove and beans (tightly packed). Pour the hot brine into the jars, leaving ½-inch (1 cm) of headspace at the top. The beans must be fully submerged in the hot brine.

Seal the hot jars, according to the manufacturer's directions. Process the jars in the boiling water canner for 15 minutes.

Storage: Enjoy at any point, but use within 1 year.

HOMEMADE MAYONNAISE

Makes about 1 cup (250 mL)

I first tasted really good mayo in France. We were hosting a party and a French couple arrived with a bowl of freshly made mayonnaise and a basket of steamed artichokes. The mayonnaise was bright yellow and silky smooth, and we spent the afternoon in the outdoor kitchen dipping the artichoke leaves into the luscious concoction. Homemade mayo makes everything it touches better. Try it on Dagwood Sandwiches (page 54) or in the Tartar Sauce (page 168).

2 egg yolks	½ tsp (2.5 mL) Worcestershire sauce
1½ Tbsp (22.5 mL) Dijon mustard	½ tsp (2.5 mL) fine sea salt
½ Tbsp (7.5 mL) fresh lemon juice	½ cup (125 mL) grape seed oil
½ Tbsp (7.5 mL) red wine vinegar	½ cup (125 mL) extra-virgin olive oil

BLEND ALL OF the ingredients except the oils in a food processor fitted with a metal blade. With the motor running, begin adding the oil in drops through the feed tube. Continue adding the oil very slowly. This process can take up to 5 minutes. The mixture should be a smooth and creamy consistency.

Transfer the mayonnaise to a clean airtight container and refrigerate until needed.

Storage: The mayonnaise can be stored, covered, in the refrigerator for up to 5 weeks.

> If I could say just one thing about making homemade mayo, I'd remind you to add the oils very slowly and thoroughly.

CHICKEN STOCK

Makes 16 cups (4 L)

One of the most useful ingredients you can have on hand, chicken stock is easy to make and should be considered part of the routine when you are cooking a whole chicken for dinner. For more inspiration on making chicken stock, see my thoughts below.

bones and drippings from a Basted
    Beer-Can Chicken (page 165) or
    store-bought roasted chicken
3 onions, unpeeled and quartered
3 carrots, chopped roughly
2 celery stalks, chopped roughly

1 bunch parsley
1 bay leaf
1 tsp (5 mL) whole peppercorns
1 Tbsp (15 mL) sea salt
20 cups (5 L) cold water

PLACE THE BONES and drippings from the cooked chicken in a large stockpot, along with the onions, carrots, celery, herbs and spices. Fill the pot with the cold water and bring to a boil.

Reduce the heat and simmer for 2–3 hours. Let the stock come to room temperature and refrigerate for a few hours or overnight.

Remove the fat from the top of the stock and strain out all of the solids. Fill airtight containers with the stock and refrigerate for up to 5 days or freeze for up to 6 months.

MY THOUGHTS ON MAKING CHICKEN STOCK There is so much flavour in stock made from a roasted chicken, and you have the bonus of enjoying a great dinner as well.

If I would rather make chicken stock the next day instead of right after we've eaten our chicken dinner, I cover the bones and drippings and refrigerate the whole thing for up to 3 days, until I'm ready to get back into the kitchen.

If you are preparing a recipe with chicken that has already been cut up into pieces, you may want to consider cutting up whole chickens (you can also ask your butcher) and saving the backs and necks to use for stock. I freeze the extra bits of chicken that I can't use for anything else, and when I have 3–4 lb (1.5–1.8 kg) collected I roast everything in the oven for an hour at 400°F (200°C). This can then be used in place of bones and drippings with the stock recipe above.

Some recipes that call for chicken stock are:

Lentil and Carrot Soup, page 49
Chicken Soup with Rice, page 48
Alphabet Soup, page 50
Broccoli-Cheddar Soup, page 70
Curried Coconut Chicken Soup, page 68
Soft Polenta, page 114

Watsa's Rice Pilau, page 115
Beef Stroganoff, page 128
Mixed Mushroom Risotto, page 144
Braised Lamb Shanks, page 160
Chicken and Dumplings, page 162

VEGGIE STOCK

Makes 16 cups (4 L)

Roasting the vegetables beforehand ensures a dark golden stock with a rich veggie flavour. If your vegetable stock is well seasoned, it makes a perfectly good vegetarian substitute for chicken stock.

3 onions, unpeeled and quartered

6 stalks celery, roughly chopped

4 large carrots, roughly chopped

4 whole tomatoes, roughly chopped

1 green pepper, seeded, cored and chopped

12 mushrooms, roughly chopped

2 Tbsp (30 mL) olive oil

3 garlic cloves, peeled and roughly chopped

1 bay leaf

2 prunes

1 Tbsp (15 mL) sea salt

1 tsp (5 mL) black peppercorns

1 bunch parsley

20 cups (5 L) cold water

PREHEAT THE OVEN to 425°F (220°C). Line a large baking sheet with parchment paper.

Toss the onions, celery, carrots, tomatoes, green pepper and mushrooms on the baking sheet and drizzle with the olive oil. Roast for about 1 hour until the vegetables have started to turn golden brown and the onions start to caramelize.

Place the browned veggies, garlic, bay leaf, prunes, salt, peppercorns and parsley in a large stockpot. Add the cold water. Bring to a boil. Reduce the heat to a simmer. Cook, uncovered, for about 2 hours.

Strain the stock and discard the solids. Let the stock come to room temperature. Fill airtight containers with the stock and refrigerate for up to 5 days or freeze for up to 6 months.

Drinks

Orangeade *256*

Rhubarb-Vanilla Soda *259*

Rhubarb Gin and Tonic *260*

Sparkling Clementine *261*

Hot Toddy *261*

Hot Cocoa with Minty Marshmallows *262*

Chai Tea *265*

Creamy Iced Coffee *266*

. . . .

ORANGEADE

Makes 8 cups (2 L)

I'm forever encouraging my kids not to reach for cans of pop/soda when we are out and about. At home, it's easier to keep the refrigerator stocked with other drink choices and this recipe is a happy compromise. Homemade orange syrup mixed with club soda is very refreshing.

3 lemons

3 oranges

2 cups (500 mL) water

1 cup (250 mL) granulated sugar

5 cups (1.25 L) club soda

PEEL THE ZEST off of the lemons and oranges with a veggie peeler or a sharp knife. Place all of the zest into a medium saucepan with the water and sugar. Bring the mixture to a boil. Reduce the heat to low and simmer for 15 minutes. Remove from the heat.

Juice the lemons and oranges and add the juice to the syrup. Stir to combine and chill in the refrigerator until cold.

Combine the chilled syrup and club soda together in a large pitcher and serve over ice.

> **VARIATION** A splash of vodka turns orangeade into a summer party drink. Garnish with a twist of orange peel.

RHUBARB-VANILLA SODA

Serves 1

Rhubarb is the first vegetable (yes, it's considered a vegetable) to come up in gardens across Canada, signalling the start of the growing season. I greedily harvest my own rhubarb patch, as well as my neighbour's, and what I don't use in pies I turn into Rhubarb-Vanilla Syrup for drinks. You may have some people say that they don't like rhubarb, but it's been my experience that this drink will have those naysayers oohing and ahhing.

ice cubes

¾ cup (185 mL) Rhubarb-Vanilla Syrup

¾ cup (185 mL) sparkling water or club soda

1 fresh strawberry for garnish

FILL A TALL glass with ice cubes. Pour the rhubarb-vanilla syrup over the ice and mix with the sparkling water or club soda. Stir well and garnish with a strawberry or a piece of mint. Serve immediately.

RHUBARB-VANILLA SYRUP

Makes 4 cups (1 L)

4 lb (1.8 kg) fresh or frozen rhubarb

3 cups (750 mL) granulated sugar

2 Tbsp (30 mL) fresh lemon juice

1 Tbsp (15 mL) pure vanilla extract

IF YOU ARE using fresh rhubarb, add 1½ cups (375 mL) water to a stockpot with the rhubarb. If you are using frozen rhubarb, allow the rhubarb to thaw in a large stockpot and proceed with the recipe.

Add the sugar and lemon juice. Bring the mixture to a boil over medium heat and stir frequently. Simmer the rhubarb mixture for about 15 minutes over medium-low heat, or until the liquid has thickened into loose syrup. Strain the syrup with a fine-mesh strainer. Discard the rhubarb pulp. Add the vanilla and chill the syrup in the refrigerator until needed.

Storage: This syrup will keep in an airtight container in the refrigerator for up to 3 weeks.

RHUBARB ORANGE BLOSSOM SYRUP Follow the recipe above but omit the vanilla and add ½ tsp (2.5 mL) orange blossom water.

ROSY RHUBARB SYRUP Follow the recipe above but omit the vanilla and add 1 tsp (5 mL) of rose water.

RHUBARB GIN AND TONIC

Serves 1

I became a gin and tonic fan while I was working at a chateau in France. We were having a break from cooking and gardening and someone gave me a tall, icy G&T while I was loung- ing in the pool, surrounded by lavender hedges. I was hooked!

Adding the Rhubarb-Vanilla Syrup to a G&T gives the classic drink a real twist. Serve as your signature cocktail at a spring party.

ice cubes

1½ oz (45 mL) good-quality gin

2 Tbsp (30 mL) Rhubarb-Vanilla Syrup
  (page 259)

¾ cup (185 mL) cold tonic water

fresh lime

PLACE 2 OR 3 ice cubes in a highball glass. Pour the gin and the rhubarb syrup into the glass and stir until combined. Slowly pour the tonic water into the glass and stir well. Garnish with a small wedge of lime. Serve with a straw.

SPARKLING CLEMENTINE

Serves 1

Greet your guests at the door with glasses of this citrusy cocktail for an extra special break-fast or brunch. If you're not in the mood for lots of company, a glass of Sparkling Clementine can make breakfast in bed a memorable occasion for two.

ice cubes
½ cup (125 mL) freshly squeezed
  clementine juice

½ cup (125 mL) chilled sparkling wine
  or champagne
1 or 2 clementine segments, for
  garnishing

FILL A CHILLED wine glass or champagne flute with ice. Pour the juice over the ice. Carefully top with the sparkling wine or champagne. Serve with a segment or 2 of clementines floating in the glass.

VARIATION For a classic mimosa, substitute the clementine juice with freshly squeezed orange juice and add 1 Tbsp (15 mL) orange liqueur.

HOT TODDY

Serves 1

For someone battling flu-like symptoms, a hot toddy has 3 main elements: the lemon for vita-min C, the honey to soothe and the alcohol to lull you to sleep. My husband is the hot toddy maker in our house, which is convenient when I'm under the weather.

1½ oz (45 mL) rum
juice of 1 lemon

1 Tbsp (15 mL) honey
1 cup (250 mL) boiling water

STIR THE RUM, lemon juice and honey together in a teacup. Add the boiling water and mix well. Serve immediately and then go to bed.

HOT COCOA WITH MINTY MARSHMALLOWS

Serves 2 lucky people

Many Canadian families spend their winter weekends on ski hills or in arenas. Wherever you find yourself, winter afternoons are made for hot cocoa. It's perfect when it's not too sweet and not too rich. Add the crème de menthe (adults only) and the minty marshmallows and you have a real treat on your hands.

2 cups (500 mL) whole milk	pinch fine sea salt
3 Tbsp (45 mL) good quality cocoa powder	¼ cup (60 mL) crème de menthe (optional)
2 Tbsp (30 mL) granulated sugar	Minty Marshmallows

WHISK THE MILK, cocoa, sugar and salt in a medium saucepan. Bring the mixture to a boil, whisking occasionally to make sure there are no lumps. Remove the pan from the heat and stir in the crème de menthe (if desired). Divide the cocoa into 2 mugs. Place 1 or 2 marshmallows in the hot cocoa. Serve immediately to a couple lucky people on a cold afternoon.

MINTY MARSHMALLOWS

Makes 9 squares

⅓ cup (80 mL) icing sugar
⅓ cup (80 mL) cornstarch
1 Tbsp (15 mL) unflavoured powdered gelatin
⅓ cup (80 mL) water
⅔ cup (160 mL) granulated sugar
½ cup (125 mL) corn syrup
½ tsp (2.5 mL) peppermint extract

LINE THE BOTTOM of an 8-inch (20 cm) square baking pan with parchment paper. Butter the parchment paper and the sides of the pan. Sift the icing sugar and cornstarch together in a small bowl. Sprinkle about 2 Tbsp (30 mL) of the mixture into the pan and tilt the pan to coat the bottom and sides.

Combine the gelatin with the water in a small saucepan and let it soak for 5 minutes.

Add the granulated sugar to the saucepan and cook over low heat until the liquid is clear.

Combine the corn syrup and peppermint extract with the warmed gelatin mixture in the bowl of a stand mixer fitted with the whisk attachment. Beat on high for 15 minutes.

Spread the marshmallow mixture in the prepared pan and smooth the top. Let stand for at least 2 hours. Dust the top with ¼ cup (60 mL) of the icing sugar-cornstarch mixture. Cut the marshmallows into 9 squares with a wet knife and roll them in the remaining icing sugar-cornstarch mixture.

Place the marshmallows on a rack and cover with paper towels. Let stand overnight to dry the surface.

Storage: Store in an airtight container for up to 1 week.

VANILLA MARSHMALLOWS Omit the peppermint extract and add 1 tsp (5 mL) pure vanilla extract instead.

·········

CHAI TEA

Makes 6 cups (1.5 L)

One of the great things about being in India is the constant availability of chai tea. Tea sellers, known as chai-wallahs, walk around streets, train stations and anywhere people are milling about, selling their hot and spicy milk tea. When at home, I like to have a pot of chai on the stove or in the refrigerator that I can reheat throughout the day, as needed.

4 cups (1 L) water

4 tea bags, your favourite black tea

3 Tbsp (45 mL) granulated sugar

25 green cardamom pods, lightly crushed but no need to destroy the shell

½ vanilla bean, split and seeds scraped out for another use (try Vanilla Bean Tapioca Pudding, page 88)

two 4-inch (10 cm) pieces cinnamon

1 tsp (5 mL) fennel seeds

5 whole cloves

3 cups (750 mL) whole milk

PLACE ALL OF the ingredients, except the milk, into a large saucepan. Bring the ingredients to a boil, reduce heat and simmer for about 5 minutes. Add the milk and bring back to a boil. Remove from the heat and strain the chai into a teapot or straight into mugs. Serve hot.

> **VARIATION** If you don't have 1 or 2 of the spices above, you can still make chai. As long as you have cinnamon and cardamom pods, you have the start of a delicious cup of chai. There are a lot of packaged chai drink mixes and syrups out there but I think once you see how easy it is to make your own, you'll forget about the rest.
>
> Barry's Irish Tea is my tea of choice for chai, as well as my regular "cuppa". It is a full-bodied, stand-your-spoon-up-in-it brew that never fails to bolster my spirits.

CREAMY ICED COFFEE

Makes 12 cups

When a certain popular coffee spot first introduced their famous icy blended coffee drink, I was living in Vancouver with a wicked habit for them. Eventually I wised up (financially and calorically) and nowadays I treat myself to my own iced coffee. Serve mid-afternoon under a shady tree while reading a good cookbook (for suggestions, see page 277).

12 cups (3 L) freshly brewed strong coffee (1 pot)

¾ cup (185 mL) sweetened condensed milk (approx)

ice cubes

2 cups (500 mL) half-and-half cream

COMBINE THE COFFEE and ¾ cup (185 mL) sweetened condensed milk. Add more sweetened condensed milk if you like it sweeter. Chill the mixture until cold.

To serve, fill a glass (or glasses) with ice cubes (see below). Pour the coffee mixture over the ice cubes, leaving enough room for cream. Pour about ¼ cup (60 mL) cream, more or less, into each glass and serve immediately with a straw.

Storage: Keep the leftover coffee mixture, covered, in the refrigerator for up to 5 days.

To make coffee ice cubes, chill leftover strong coffee until cold. Pour into an ice cube tray and freeze until firm.

THE COFFEE RUN

One gray, drizzly summer's day, we were on our boat, docked out in the islands just off of Gananoque, Ontario. I could have made coffee on board but the lure of a really good espresso drink had gotten stuck in my head, so the four of us got into our little zodiac and headed into town. To save ourselves some time, we pulled up to a grassy embankment on the river just behind the cafe we were aiming for. Alan told me that I'd have to jump out of the boat and climb the bank to secure the rope to a tree. He made it sound easy. I threw myself off of the front of the zodiac and landed like an oversized spider on the wet grass, screaming and clinging to the bank for dear life. My family rolled with laughter as I inched myself up the hill. By the time I finally got the rope secured, I was muddy, grass-stained and dishevelled beyond belief. But I enjoyed every bit of my Americano.

Odds and Ends

Finger Paints   *270*
Salty Watercolours   *271*
Very Cherry Play Dough   *272*
Peanut Butter and Honey Bones   *274*
Knitted Dish Cloth   *276*

FINGER PAINTS

Makes about 6 cups (1.5 L)

My Grandma Smith has always loved painting. I picture her using paints like these as a child. These days my kids do double duty with these paints and Salty Watercolours—they help to make them and then create art with them. We usually whip up a batch or two of finger paints when my nephew and niece, Hugh and Erica, come to visit. These are particularly good for little ones because they don't contain harmful chemicals.

1 cup (250 mL) all-purpose flour	3 cups (750 mL) boiling water
1 cup (250 mL) cold water	food colouring pastes

COMBINE THE FLOUR with the cold water in a medium saucepan until smooth. Add the boiling water and bring to boil over high heat, stirring constantly. Remove from the heat.

Divide the mixture into small bowls, depending on how many colours you wish to mix up.

Add a little bit of food colouring to each bowl and stir thoroughly. For darker colours, add more food colouring.

Make sure your artists are wearing painting clothes and let them create their masterpieces using their fingers and hands.

Storage: Store paints in the refrigerator for up to 1 week.

You can always add more food colouring, but you can't take it away once you've mixed it in. Start with a small amount and work your way up.

SALTY WATERCOLOURS

Makes 3 Tbsp (45 mL) of 1 colour

My daughter Ellen showed me how to make these paints. When dry, the paintings sparkle. Keep a wide variety of food colours on hand and you'll be able to create paintings in every colour of the rainbow.

3 Tbsp (45 mL) boiling water   food colouring pastes
1 Tbsp (15 mL) table salt

COMBINE THE BOILING water and salt in a small dish. Swish the mixture around until the salt is almost all dissolved. Add a little dab of food colouring paste and mix well. Repeat the process for as many colours as you like.

Storage: These paints will keep indefinitely in an airtight container at room temperature.

VERY CHERRY PLAY DOUGH

Makes 3 cups (750 mL)

When I was looking for a great play dough recipe, I checked in with my friend, Jennifer, a teacher who truly loves what she does. She uses this recipe in her classroom as it doesn't need any cooking, just boiling water. Not only is this play dough fun to play with, it smells really good, too. Almost good enough to eat.

2½ cups (625 mL) all-purpose flour
½ cup (125 mL) table salt
2 Tbsp (30 mL) cream of tartar
1½ cups (375 mL) boiling water

two 0.2 oz (6 g) packages cherry-flavoured drink crystals
3 Tbsp (45 mL) vegetable oil

COMBINE THE FLOUR, salt and cream of tartar together in the bowl of a stand mixer fitted with the paddle attachment.

Mix the boiling water with the drink crystals in a small bowl and stir until completely dissolved. Add the vegetable oil.

Pour the liquid mixture into the dry ingredients and blend on medium speed for about 3 minutes, until the dough has completely come together. Remove the dough from the mixer bowl and knead until it is perfectly smooth.

Storage: Keep the play dough in an airtight container for up to 2 weeks.

PEANUT BUTTER AND HONEY BONES

Makes about 4 dozen 3-inch (8 cm) bones

These biscuits are based on a recipe given to me by the owner of Poochini's Barkery, a local doggy store that makes biscuits in all sorts of shapes and flavours. Our golden retriever, Oscar, loves peanut butter. And nothing is too good for Oscar.

2 cups (500 mL) whole-wheat flour
1 cup (250 mL) all-purpose flour
1 cup (250 mL) rye or barley flour
3 eggs, slightly beaten
½ cup (125 mL) vegetable oil

¼ cup (60 mL) peanut butter
¼ cup (60 mL) honey
¼ cup (60 mL) water, plus a little
   more if necessary

PREHEAT THE OVEN to 300°F (150°C). Line a large baking sheet with parchment paper.

Place all of the dry ingredients in the work bowl of a stand mixer fitted with a paddle attachment.

Whisk the eggs, oil, peanut butter, honey and water together in a medium bowl. Slowly pour the wet ingredients into the dry ingredients with the mixer on low speed. Continue mixing the dough until it comes together and is moist enough to roll out. Add another 1 or 2 Tbsp (15–30 mL) of water if necessary.

Divide the dough into 4 pieces. Roll each piece out to about ¼-inch (6 mm) thick on a piece of parchment paper with a lightly floured rolling pin. Cut into dog-friendly shapes (I like the traditional dog-bone shape or a variety of farm animals). Reroll the scraps. Repeat with the remaining dough.

Bake for about 45 minutes or until the biscuits are golden and crunchy.

Storage: Keep the biscuits in an airtight container for up to 2 months.

KNITTED DISH CLOTH

Makes 2

I love knitting and this is one of the easiest projects to do while sitting in front of a rerun Downton Abbey *episode or while being a passenger on a long road trip.*

1 skein cotton yarn (makes about 2 cloths)

1 pair size 6 or 7 needles

CAST ON 4 stitches. Knit one row.

Row 1: Knit

Row 2: K2, yarn over, knit across row

Repeat row 2 until 48 stitches are on the needle. Decrease as follows: At beginning of row knit 1, knit 2 together, yarn over, knit 2 together, knit across. Repeat this decrease row until 4 stitches remain. Bind off.

MY FAVOURITE COOKBOOKS

"A pudding as comforting as an old teddy bear."

— From the book *Ripe* by Nigel Slater describing a recipe for
Warm Rice Pudding with Cinnamon, Apple and Maple Syrup.

I have a friend who believes that if she cooks two or three recipes from a cookbook, it's been worth the cost of the book. Not every cookbook I own has "paid its way" according to this criteria, but many have. There are cookbooks acquired on trips and travels that are kept around for the memories. There are cookbooks that are more for reading and cookbooks that are used for more practical purposes. There are those that I have because I should have them in my collection, and little known books that I have just because I love them.

I have always loved cookbooks. My passion for cookbooks led me to go back to school to become a chef and it has always informed the way I cook. I am no longer a cook in a restaurant, but I'm still an avid cookbook reader.

There are lots of cookbooks published every year but I'm still very attached to some of my old standbys. Here is a list, some newer and some older, of my favourite cookbooks. These are books that I have read, reread, cooked from, recommended, given as gifts and generally enjoyed over the years. Take this list to your library or local bookstore and see if you agree with me.

The Complete Canadian Living Cookbook by Elizabeth Baird:
If you live in Canada, you need this Canadian standard. Mine is food-spattered and dog-eared.

Rose's Christmas Cookies by Rose Levy Beranbaum: A book that gets me in the holiday spirit every year. Rose's recipes are very well written.

Better Homes and Gardens New Cookbook: The iconic red and white checked cover of this book reminds me of my youth.

Continued . . .

MY FAVOURITE COOKBOOKS
(continued)

Cold-Weather Cooking by Sarah Leah Chase: One of my all-time favourite cookbooks, Sarah Chase was ahead of her time and her cookbooks are full of truly delicious comfort food.

Home Cooking by Laurie Colwin: A book of essays on food and life, plus recipes. I love her writing and her follow-up, *More Home Cooking*, is just as good. Both books tied up in ribbon make for a great gift.

River Cottage Preserves Handbook by Pam Corbin: I love this little English book for preserving inspiration.

Good Tempered Food by Tamasin Day-Lewis: This is a book that inspires me every time I crack the cover.

Out to Brunch At Mildred Pierce Restaurant by Donna Dooher: A small cookbook full of great recipes that will have you inviting people over for brunch as soon as possible.

Barefoot Contessa Family Style by Ina Garten: My most-used Barefoot Contessa book. Everything I've made from this book hits the spot.

Bills: Breakfast, Lunch + Dinner by Bill Granger: An inspiring book from a popular Australian restaurant owner. I love the simplicity and ideas in this book.

Baking: From My Home to Yours by Dorie Greenspan: This book makes me want to get up off my duff and into the kitchen to start baking.

Salt Sugar Smoke by Diana Henry: Everything that I want in a preserving book.

Artisan Bread in Five Minutes a Day by Jeff Hertzberg and Zoë François: The recipes in this book inspired several of my bread-making classes.

The Essential New York Times Cookbook by Amanda Hesser: Truly essential, I love Amanda Hesser's writing in this desert island book.

The Rose and Thistle Tea Room Cook Book by Mary Leach: The first cookbook that I started cooking from in earnest. I've made almost everything in this book.

The Farmhouse Cookbook by Susan Herrmann Loomis: Great stories and wonderful recipes. She also wrote *On Rue Tatin*.

Hollyhocks & Radishes: Mrs. Chard's Almanac Cookbook by Bonnie Stewart Mickelson: A charming book from northern Michigan. Reading this cookbook is like getting a hug from your grandmother.

Inn on the Twenty Cookbook by Anna and Michael Olson: A book that I turn to again and again, we used this book for our wedding guests to sign. Did I mention that Anna actually made our wedding cake? Aren't we lucky!

The Village Baker's Wife by Gayle and Joe Ortiz and Louisa Beers: A wonderful baking book that everyone who loves baking should own.

Plenty by Yotam Ottolenghi: One of the most inspiring vegetarian cookbooks I've cooked from. The recipes are as delicious as the pictures make them out to be.

The Bombay Cafe by Neela Paniz: This was a recommendation from a well-known Canadian restaurateur and it has served me well through my forays into Indian cooking.

The Harrow Fair Cookbook by Moira Sanders, Lori Elstone and Beth Goslin Maloney: Aside from the fact that I co-wrote this little gem, it's the sort of cookbook that you'll pick up over and over.

Patricia Wells At Home in Provence by Patricia Wells: A book that I was fortunate to have with me when I was living in France, it's full of straight-forward French recipes.

MENU IDEAS

CANADA DAY PICNIC SAILBOAT CHICKEN (page 140) · *Summer Bean Salad* (page 44) · CORN ON THE COB WITH ROASTED TOMATO BUTTER (page 118) · *Grilled Bread* (page 100) · RANGER COOKIES (page 81)

KID'S BIRTHDAY PARTY VEGGIE PLATE WITH BLUE CHEESE DIP (page 94) · *Homemade Pizza* (page 148) · ROMAINE SALAD WITH CREAMY ITALIAN DRESSING AND FRESH GARLIC CROUTONS (page 62) · *Orange Birthday Cake* (page 194)

INDIAN DINNER MY FAVOURITE CHICKEN CURRY (page 136) · *Watsa's Rice Pilau* (page 115) · CUCUMBERS IN YOGURT (page 116) · *Steamed Carrot Pudding* (page 212) · CHAI TEA (page 265)

WINTER BRUNCH SHIRRED EGGS WITH MAPLE BACON (page 23) · *Cheddar and Red Onion Biscuits* (page 27) · OLD-FASHIONED SOUR CREAM COFFEE CAKE (page 30) · *Sparkling Clementine* (page 261)

ROAD TRIP DAGWOOD SANDWICHES (page 54) · *Peanut Butter Chocolate Squares* (page 91) · RHUBARB-VANILLA SODAS (page 259)

BAKE SALE LAVENDER SHORTBREAD JAM SANDWICHES (page 83) • *Animal Crackers* (page 84) • RASPBERRY CREAM CHEESE BROWNIES (page 179) • *Stamped Shortbread Cookies* (page 187) • APPLE STRUDEL (page 191)

MOVIE NIGHT FRESH TORTILLA CHIPS WITH GUACAMOLE (page 98) • *Lamb Burgers with Yogurt-Cucumber Spread* (page 132) • KALE TABBOULEH (page 67) • *Banana Splits with (Moira) Sanders Hot Fudge Sauce* (page 184)

CELEBRATORY DINNER WARM OLIVES (page 95) • *Rhubarb Gin and Tonics* (page 260) • SUNDAY ROAST BEEF TENDERLOIN (page 152) • *Cabbage and Mashed Yukon Gold Potatoes* (page 110) • PAN-FRIED BRUSSELS SPROUTS WITH MAPLE SYRUP AND BACON (page 121) • *Individual Baked Alaskas* (page 206)

DINNER WITH FRIENDS RETRO CHEESE BALL (page 102) • *Chicken with Dried Plums and Green Olives* (page 135) • SOFT POLENTA (page 114) • *Roasted Cauliflower* (page 122) • BUTTERSCOTCH CREAM PIE (page 208)

BOOK CLUB PROSCIUTTO-FETA BITES (page 107) • *Edamame Spread with Crostini* (page 96) • DOUBLE VANILLA POUND CAKE (page 176) • *Pretzel Caramels* (page 89)

A BIG THANK YOU . . .

ALAN, GAVIN AND ELLEN SANDERS • CHUCK AND SHARON MCDONALD • LORI, JAKE, HUGH AND ERICA ELSTONE • BETH GOSLIN MALONEY • MAX SANDERS • ADRIAN STOCKING / WWW.WILLOWIND.CA • ANNIE LAWTON SCURFIELD • ALLANA HARKIN • BETH STEVENSON / WWW.BRAINPOWER-STUDIO.COM • BHARATH KUMAR REDDY AND FAMILY • BRENDA JASMIN • CAROL JENNER • CHRISTINE STEWART • DANIELLE STE. MARIE • DIANE AND TOM INGERSOLL • DIANE EVANS • DONREY MACINTOSH • ELAINE AND DERMOT FEORE • EVIE KOZLESKI • FIONA STEVENSON • FRAN JENNER • HARROW FAIR BOARD • HERBIE JONES • ISA MOTTIER • JAMIE WALDRON AND ERIN GARDNER • JANETTE LAWTON • JENNIFER BIRTLES • JESSE MARCHAND • JOE AND ALBA FORNO • JOHN AND CAROL VADEIKA • JOY BLOOMFIELD • KAREN ARMSTRONG • KARLA WILSON / WWW.HAVENCON-TEMPORARY.COM • KATHERINE BELROSE • KATHY WURFEL • KRISTINE NEWMAN • KRISTIN MERZ • LEA LAUZON • LEE WADDINGTON • MARGARET WATSA • MARGUERITE AND MARC MANTHA • MARIE HALL • MELANIE PILKINGTON • MICHELLE BRUNET / WWW.UNWINDYARNHOUSE.COM • MICHELLE FURBACHER • MIKE MCCOLL • NANCY AND BRIAN LEONARD • NANCY SERRICK • NICK RUNDALL • PAULEEN CUSACK • PETRA MARTLOCK • RITA PORFIRIS • SHAILA VISSER • SHARON HOPE UNITED CHURCH • SILOAM ORCHARDS / WWW.SILOAMORCHARDS.COM • STEVE AND LISA COOPER / WWW.COOPERSFARM.CA • SUSAN MCGINN • TARA MEYER

INDEX

A

A Chicken Story in India, 139
All-Season Tomato Sauce, 247
Animal Crackers, 84
Alphabet Soup, 50
appetizers
    Blue Cheese Dip, 94
    Cheesy Spinach and Apple
      Squares, 106
    Crostini, 96
    Edamame Spread, 96
    Fresh Sesame Bread Sticks, 105
    Fresh Tortilla Chips with
      Guacamole, 98
    Grilled Bread, 100
    Proscuitto-Feta Bites, 107
    Retro Cheese Ball, 102
    Warm Olives, 95
apples. *See also* crab apples
    Apple Pie Folly, 224
    Apple Strudel, 191
    Apple-Pear Pie, 225
    Baked Apples, 210
    Puffy Apple Pancake, 26
apricots
    White Chocolate Apricot Scones,
      29
Arrowroot Flour, 84
asparagus
    Asparagus and Ham Quiche, 41
avocado
    Fresh Tortilla Chips with
      Guacamole, 98

B

bacon
    Bacon, How to Cook, 61
    Grilled Chicken and Double
      Smoked Bacon Salad, 61
    Maple Bacon, 23
    Pan-Fried Brussels Sprouts with
      Maple Syrup and Bacon, 121
    Roasted Peameal Bacon, 36

bagels
    Montreal-style Bagels, 13
    Veggie Cream Cheese on, 13
Baked Alaskas, Individual, 206
Baked Apples, 210
Baked Mac and Cheese, 75
bananas
    Banana Split, 184
    Chocolate Banana Layer Cake with
      Banana Buttercream, 198
barbecue
    Basted Beer-Can Chicken, 165
    Cheesy Potato Casserole with
      Grilled Sausages, 38
    Hand-Pressed Chicken Burger
      Patties, 71
    Lamb Burgers with Yogurt-
      Cucumber Spread, 132
    Ribs with Chuck's Barbecue Sauce,
      158
    Sailboat Chicken, 140
Barry's Irish Tea, 265
Basmati Rice, Perfect, 53
beans
    Pickled Green Beans, 249
    Summer Bean Salad, 44
    White Bean and Tomato Linguini, 145
beef
    Beef Stroganoff, 128
    Cottage Pie, 130
    Meatballs, 129
    Meatloaf, 129
    Sunday Roast Beef Tenderloin, 152
Beer-Can Chicken, Basted, 165
berries. *See* blueberries; raspberries;
    strawberries
Birthday Cake, Orange, 194
biscuits. *See* breads and biscuits
Black and Blue Jam, 238
blueberries
    Black and Blue Jam, 238
    Peach-Blueberry Cobbler, 181
    Wild Blueberry Pie, 227
blue cheese

Blue Cheese Dip, 94
Bones, Peanut Butter and Honey, 274
Braised Lamb Shanks, 160
bread (as ingredient)
    Cinnamon Butter on Toast, 12
    Crostini, 96
    Grilled Bread, 100
    Jammy Bread Pudding, 33
    Veggie Cream Cheese on Bagels, 13
bread crumbs
    Caramelized Bread Crumb Ice
      Cream, 211
    Dry Bread Crumbs, 71
    Fresh Bread Crumbs, 71
breads & biscuits. *See also* muffins
    Cheddar and Red Onion Biscuits, 27
    Fresh Sesame Bread Sticks, 105
    Soda Bread with Dried Cherries, 117
    Sweet Potato and Zucchini Bread,
      32
breakfast and brunch
    Asparagus and Ham Quiche, 41
    Buttermilk Pancakes, 19
    Carrot-Ginger Muffins, 14
    Cheddar and Red Onion Biscuits,
      27
    Cheesy Potato Casserole with
      Grilled Sausages, 38
    Cherry Crumble Oatmeal, 8
    Cinnamon Butter on Toast, 12
    Egg Cups and Toast Shapes, 20
    Egg-In-The-Hole, 22
    French Crumpets, 11
    Ginger Quinoa Granola, 6
    Homemade Pancake Mix, 19
    Jammy Bread Pudding, 33
    Old-Fashioned Sour Cream Coffee
      Cake, 30
    Overnight Pumpkin Waffles, 34
    Puffy Apple Pancake, 26
    Roasted Peameal Bacon, 36
    Shirred Eggs with Maple Bacon, 23
    Strawberry Oatmeal Muffins, 16
    Sweet Breakfast Custards, 9

breakfast and brunch (cont'd)
  Sweet Potato and Zucchini Bread, 32
  Turkey Sausage Patties, 37
  Veggie Cream Cheese for Bagels, 13
  White Chocolate Apricot Scones, 29
broccoli
  Broccoli with Cheddar Cheese Sauce, 125
  Broccoli-Cheddar Soup, 70
brownies
  Raspberry Cream Cheese Brownies, 179
brunch. See breakfast & brunch
Brussels Sprouts, Pan-Fried with Maple Syrup and Bacon, 121
Bubble-Gum Ice Cream, 182
burgers
  Hand-Pressed Chicken Burger Patties, 71
  Lamb Burgers with Yogurt-Cucumber Spread, 132
butter
  Chive Flower Butter, 101
  Honeycomb Butter, 11
  Cinnamon Butter on Toast, 12
  Roasted Tomato Butter, 120
Buttercream, Banana, 198
buttermilk
  Buttermilk Pancakes, 19
butterscotch
  Butterscotch Cream Pie, 208
  Butterscotch Sauce, 213

C
cabbage
  Cabbage and Mashed Yukon Gold Potatoes, 110
  Cabbage Rolls, 154
cakes. See also cupcakes
  Caramelized Pear Gingerbread Cake, 177
  Chocolate Banana Layer Cake with Banana Buttercream, 196
  Double Vanilla Pound Cake, 176
  Old-Fashioned Sour Cream Coffee Cake, 30
  Orange Birthday Cake, 194

Pumpkin Cheesecake, 203
candied ginger
  Ginger Quinoa Granola, 6
candy
  Peanut Butter Chocolate Squares, 91
  Pretzel Caramels, 89
canning. See preserves
caramel
  Pretzel Caramels, 89
  Caramelized Bread Crumb Ice Cream, 211
Carrots
  Baked Carrots with Horseradish, 123
  Carrot-Ginger Muffins, 14
  Lentil and Carrot Soup, 52
  Steamed Carrot Pudding, 212
Caramelized Pear Gingerbread Cake, 177
cauliflower
  Roasted Cauliflower, 122
Chai Tea, 265
Charcoal Grilling, 164
cheddar cheese
  Baked Mac and Cheese, 75
  Broccoli with Cheddar Cheese Sauce, 125
  Broccoli-Cheddar Soup, 70
  Cheddar and Red Onion Biscuits, 27
  Cheesy Potato Casserole with Grilled Sausages, 38
  Cheesy Spinach and Apple Squares, 106
  Grilled Pimento-Cheese Sandwiches, 72
cheese. See blue cheese; cheddar cheese; cream cheese; goat cheese; mozzarella; Parmesan cheese; Swiss cheese
Cheesecake, Pumpkin, 203
Cheese Ball, Retro, 102
cherries
  Cherry Crumble Oatmeal, 8
  Chewy White and Dark Chocolate Chunk Cookies, 229
  Soda Bread with Dried Cherries, 117
  Very Cherry Play Dough, 272

Cherry Tomato, Fresh Corn Salad with, 47
Chewy White and Dark Chocolate Chunk Cookies, 229
Chia Seeds, 6
chicken
  A Chicken Story in India, 139
  Basted Beer-Can Chicken, 165
  Boneless, Skinless Chicken Breast, 48
  Chicken and Dumplings, 162
  Chicken Soup with Rice, 48
  Chicken Stock, 251
  Chicken Tenders with Honey-Mustard Dipping Sauce, 141
  Chicken with Dried Plums and Green Olives, 135
  Curried Coconut Chicken Soup, 68
  Grilled Chicken and Double Smoked Bacon Salad, 61
  Hand-Pressed Chicken Burger Patties, 71
  My Favourite Chicken Curry, 136
  Chicken Nuggets, 71
  Sailboat Chicken, 140
Chili Sauce with Fruit, 248
Chili Sauce, Slow-Cooker, 248
Chive Flower Butter, 101
chocolate. See also white chocolate
  Chewy White and Dark Chocolate Chunk Cookies, 229
  Chocolate Banana Layer Cake with Banana Buttercream, 198
  Chocolate Pudding, 87
  Peanut Butter Chocolate Squares, 91
Chutney, Pear-Cranberry, 244
Cinnamon Butter on Toast, 12
Clementine, Sparkling, 261
cocktails. See drinks
Cocoa, Hot with Minty Marshmallows, 262
coconut
  Curried Coconut Chicken Soup, 68
coffee
  The Coffee Run, 267
  Creamy Iced Coffee, 270
  Old-Fashioned Sour Cream Coffee

Cake, 30
Community Supported Agriculture, 2
condiments. *See also* sauces
   Homemade Mayonnaise, 250
   Pear-Cranberry Chutney, 244
cookbooks
   Artisan Bread in Five Minutes a
     Day, 278
   Baking: From My Home to Yours,
     278
   Barefoot Contessa Family Style, 278
   Better Homes and Gardens New
     Cookbook, 277
   Bills: Breakfast, Lunch + Dinner, 278
   Bombay Cafe, 279
   Cold-Weather Cooking, 278
   Complete Canadian Living
     Cookbook, 277
   Essential New York Times
     Cookbook, 279
   Farmhouse Cookbook, 279
   Good Tempered Food, 278
   Harrow Fair Cookbook, 279
   Hollyhocks & Radishes: Mrs.
     Chard's Almanac Cookbook, 279
   Home Cooking, 278
   Inn on the Twenty Cookbook, 279
   Out to Brunch At Mildred Pierce
     Restaurant, 278
   Patricia Wells At Home in
     Provence, 279
   Plenty, 279
   River Cottage Preserves
     Handbook, 278
   Rose and Thistle Tea Room
     Cookbook, 279
   Rose's Christmas Cookies, 277
   Salt Sugar Smoke, 278
   Sugar, 229
   Village Baker's Wife, 279
cookies. *See also* squares
   Chewy White and Dark Chocolate
     Chunk Cookies, 229
   Cookie Stamp, 187
   Crab Apple Crescent Cookies, 228
   Fortune Cookies, 214
   Lavender Shortbread Jam
     Sandwiches, 83
   Lemon Shortbread Jam

     Sandwiches, 83
   Malted Milk Cookies, 188
   Ranger Cookies, 81
   Stamped Shortbread Cookies, 187
   Walnut-Spice Icebox Cookies, 185
corn and cornmeal. *See also* popcorn
   Corn on the Cob with Roasted
     Tomato Butter, 118
   Fresh Corn and Cherry Tomato
     Salad, 47
Cottage Pie, 130
crab apples
   Crab Apple Crescent Cookies, 228
   Crab Apple Jelly, 240
crackers
   Animal Crackers, 84
   Saltine Crackers, 167
   Spotted Animal Crackers, 84
cranberry
   Pear-Cranberry Chutney, 244
cream cheese
   Raspberry Cream Cheese
     Brownies, 179
   Veggie Cream Cheese on Bagels, 13
Cream Pie, Butterscotch, 208
Creamy Iced Coffee, 266
Creamy Italian Dressing, 63
Crostini, 96
croutons
   Fresh Garlic Croutons, 63
Crumble, Cherry Oatmeal, 8
Crumpets, French, 11
cucumbers
   Cucumbers in Yogurt, 116
   Lamb Burgers with Yogurt-
     Cucumber Spread, 132
cupcakes
   Cupcakes, Violet, 200
Curried Coconut Chicken Soup, 68
Curry, My Favourite Chicken, 136
custard
   Sweet Breakfast Custards, 9

D
Dagwood Sandwiches, 54
deep frying
   Fresh Tortilla Chips with
     Guacamole, 98
   Perch-in-a-Basket, 166

   Shrimp-in-a-Basket, 166
desserts
   Apple Strudel, 191
   Apple-Pear Pie, 225
   Baked Apples, 210
   Bubble-Gum Ice Cream, 182
   Butterscotch Cream Pie, 208
   Caramelized Bread Crumb Ice
     Cream, 211
   Caramelized Pear Gingerbread
     Cake, 177
   Chewy White and Dark Chocolate
     Chunk Cookies, 229
   Chocolate Banana Layer Cake with
     Banana Buttercream, 198
   Crab Apple Crescent Cookies, 228
   Double Vanilla Pound Cake, 176
   Flaky Pie Dough, 222
   Fortune Cookies, 214
   Individual Baked Alaskas, 206
   Malted Milk Cookies, 188
   (Moira) Sanders Hot Fudge Sauce, 184
   Orange Birthday Cake, 194
   Peach-Blueberry Cobbler, 181
   Pumpkin Cheesecake, 203
   Raspberry Cream Cheese
     Brownies, 179
   Stamped Shortbread Cookies, 187
   Steamed Carrot Pudding, 212
   Strawberry Shortcake, 174
   Sugared Violet Blossoms, 202
   Sweet Potato Pie, 226
   Violet Cupcakes, 200
   Walnut-Spice Icebox Cookies, 185
   White Chocolate Raspberry Yule
     Log, 204
   Wild Blueberry Pie, 227
dips
   Blue Cheese Dip, 94
   Edamame Spread, 96
   Guacamole, 98
   Watercress Dip, 113
Dirty Dishes Playlist, 171
dressings and vinaigrettes. *See also*
   salads
   Creamy Italian Dressing, 63
Dried Cherries, Soda Bread, 117
drinks
   Chai Tea, 265

drinks (cont'd)
    Creamy Iced Coffee, 266
    Hot Cocoa with Minty
        Marshmallows, 262
    Hot Toddy, 261
    Mimosa, 261
    Orangeade, 256
    Rhubarb Gin and Tonic, 260
    Rhubarb-Vanilla Soda, 259
    Sparkling Clementine, 261
Dry Bread Crumbs, 71
Dumplings, Chicken and, 162

E

Edamame Spread, 96
eggs
    Egg Cups and Toast Shapes, 20
    Egg-In-The-Hole, 22
    Shirred Eggs with Maple Bacon, 23
entrees. *See* mains

F

feta cheese
    Macedonian Feta cheese, 107
    Prosciutto-Feta Bites, 107
Finger Paints, 270
fish
    Perch-In-A-Basket with Tartar
        Sauce, 166
    Seared Salmon, 142
Flaky Pie Dough, 222
Fortune Cookies, 214
Fortunes, 216-217
freezer jam
    Peach Freezer Jam, 239
    Strawberry-Vanilla Freezer Jam, 234
French Crumpets, 11
Fresh Corn and Cherry Tomato
    Salad, 47
Fresh Bread Crumbs, 71
Fresh Garlic Croutons, 63
frosting. *See* icing
frozen treats
    Bubble-Gum Ice Cream, 182
    Caramelized Bread Crumb Ice
        Cream, 211
    Individual Baked Alaskas, 206
    Strawberry Ice Pops, 86
    Strawberry Rhubarb Ice Pops, 86
Fudge Sauce, (Moira) Sanders Hot, 184

G

Garlic, Fresh Croutons, 63
Gin and Tonic, Rhubarb, 260
ginger. *See also* candied ginger
    Caramelized Pear Gingerbread
        Cake, 177
    Carrot-Ginger Muffins, 14
    Ginger Quinoa Granola, 6
goat cheese
    Goat Cheese and Herb Ravioli, 146
    Green Pea Salad with Mint and
        Goat Cheese, 64
Green Beans, Pickled, 249
Grilled Bread, 100
Grilled Chicken and Double Smoked
    Bacon Salad, 61
Grilled Pimento-Cheese Sandwiches,
    72
Guacamole, with Fresh Tortilla
    Chips, 98

H

Ham, Quiche with Asparagus, 41
hamburgers. *See* burgers
Hand Tarts, Tomato, 56
Hemp Hearts, 6
herbs
    Goat Cheese and Herb Ravioli, 146
honey
    Chicken Tenders with Honey-
        Mustard Dipping Sauce, 141
    Peanut Butter and Honey Bones,
        274
Honeycomb Butter, 11
Horseradish
    Baked Carrots with Horseradish,
        123
    Horseradish Cream, 152
Horticultural Societies, 177
Hot Cocoa with Minty
    Marshmallows, 262
Hot Toddy, 261
How to Enter a Baking Competition,
    220

I

ice cream
    Bubble-Gum Ice Cream, 182
    Caramelized Bread Crumb Ice
        Cream, 211

    Raspberry Cream-Cheese Brownie
        Ice Cream, 211
Ice Pops, Strawberry, 86
Ice Pops, Strawberry Rhubarb, 86
Icebox Cookies, Walnut-Spice, 185
Iced Coffee, Creamy, 266
icing
    Banana Buttercream, 198
    Malted Milk Frosting, 188
Individual Baked Alaskas, 206

J

jam and jelly
    Black and Blue Jam, 238
    Crab Apple Jelly, 240
    Jammy Bread Pudding, 33
    Lavender Shortbread Jam
        Sandwiches, 83
    Peach Freezer Jam, 239
    Red and Black Jam, 237
    Strawberry-Vanilla Freezer Jam,
        234
    Two-Burner Raspberry Jam, 243
Jammy Bread Pudding, 33

K

kale
    Kale Tabbouleh, 67
Kettle Corn, Home-Popped, 80
Knitted Dish Cloth, 276

L

lamb
    Braised Lamb Shanks, 160
    Lamb Burgers with Yogurt-
        Cucumber Spread, 132
lavender
    Lavender Shortbread Jam
        Sandwiches, 83
Layer Cake, Chocolate Banana with
    Banana Buttercream, 198
lemons
    Lemon Shortbread Jam
        Sandwiches, 83
lentils
    Lentil and Carrot Soup, 52
Linguini, White Bean and Tomato,
    145

M

Mac and Cheese, Baked, 75
Macedonian Feta Cheese, 107
mains
    Basted Beer-Can Chicken, 165
    Beef Stroganoff, 128
    Braised Lamb Shanks, 160
    Cabbage Rolls, 154
    Chicken and Dumplings, 162
    Chicken Tenders with Honey-
        Mustard Dipping Sauce, 141
    Chicken with Dried Plums and
        Green Olives, 135
    Cottage Pie, 130
    Goat Cheese and Herb Ravioli, 146
    Homemade Pizza, 148
    Lamb Burgers with Yogurt-
        Cucumber Spread, 132
    Meatloaf, 129
    Mixed Mushroom Risotto, 144
    My Favourite Chicken Curry, 136
    Perch-In-A-Basket with Tartar
        Sauce, 166
    Ribs with Chuck's Barbecue Sauce,
        158
    Sailboat Chicken, 140
    Seared Salmon, 142
    Stuffed Shells, 169
    Sunday Roast Beef Tenderloin, 152
    White Bean and Tomato Linguini,
        145
    Winter Meat Pies, 156
Malted Milk Cookies, 188
maple syrup
    Pan-Fried Brussels Sprouts with
        Maple Syrup and Bacon, 121
    Shirred Eggs with Maple Bacon, 23
Marshmallows, Minty with Hot
    Cocoa, 262
Marshmallows, Vanilla 263
Maslin Pan, 238
Mayonnaise, Homemade, 250
Meatballs, 129
Meatloaf, 129
menus
    Bake Sale, 281
    Book Club, 281
    Canada Day Picnic, 280
    Celebratory Dinner, 281

    Dinner With Friends, 281
    Indian Dinner, 280
    Kid's Birthday Party, 280
    Movie Night, 281
    Road Trip, 280
    Winter Brunch, 280
Mincemeat, Apple Strudel with, 191
mint
    Green Pea Salad with Mint And
        Goat Cheese, 64
    Hot Cocoa with Minty
        Marshmallows, 262
(Moira) Sanders Hot Fudge Sauce,
    184
Montreal-Style Bagels, 13
muffins
    Carrot-Ginger Muffins, 14
    Strawberry Oatmeal Muffins, 16
    Sweet Potato and Zucchini Muffins,
        32
mushrooms
    Mixed Mushroom Risotto, 144
mustard
    Chicken Tenders with Honey-
        Mustard Dipping Sauce, 141
    Mustard Sauce, with Seared
        Salmon, 142

N

Nuggets, Chicken, 71
nuts. *See* peanut butter, walnuts

O

oats
    Cherry Crumble Oatmeal, 8
    Strawberry Oatmeal Muffins, 16
odds and ends
    Finger Paints, 270
    Knitted Dish Cloth, 276
    Peanut Butter and Honey Bones,
        274
    Salty Watercolours, 271
    Very Cherry Play Dough, 272
Old-Fashioned Sour Cream Coffee
    Cake, 30
olives
    Chicken with Dried Plums and
        Green Olives, 135
    Warm Olives, 95

onions
    Cheddar and Red Onion Biscuits,
        27
oranges
    Orange Birthday Cake, 194
    Orangeade, 256
    Rhubarb Orange Blossom Syrup,
        259
Overnight Pumpkin Waffles, 34

P

paints
    Finger Paints, 270
    Salty Watercolours, 271
pancakes
    Buttermilk Pancakes, 19
    Homemade Pancake Mix, 19
    Puffy Apple Pancake, 26
Pantry Items, Preserves and, 232
pasta
    Alphabet Soup, 50
    Baked Mac and Cheese, 75
    Goat Cheese and Herb Ravioli, 146
    Stuffed Shells, 169
    White Bean and Tomato Linguini,
        145
peaches
    Peach Freezer Jam, 239
    Peach-Blueberry Cobbler, 181
Peameal Bacon, Roasted, 36
peanut butter
    Peanut Butter and Honey Bones,
        274
    Peanut Butter Chocolate Squares, 91
pears
    Apple-Pear Pie, 225
    Caramelized Pear Gingerbread
        Cake, 177
    Pear-Cranberry Chutney, 244
peas
    Green Pea Salad with Mint and
        Goat Cheese, 64
Perch-In-A-Basket with Tartar Sauce,
    166
Perchwiches, 166
Pilau, Watsa's Rice, 115
pickles
    Pickled Green Beans, 249
    Pickling Spice, 248

pies & pastry
    Apple Strudel, 191
    Asparagus and Ham Quiche, 41
    Butterscotch Cream Pie, 209
    Flaky Pie Dough, 222
    Sweet Potato Pie, 226
    Tomato Hand Tarts, 56
    Wild Blueberry Pie, 227
    Winter Meat Pies, 156
Pimento-Cheese Sandwiches, Grilled, 72
Pimento-Cheese Welsh Rarebit, 72
Pimentos, about, 73
pizza
    Homemade Pizza, 148
    Homemade Pizza Sauce, 246
Play Dough, Very Cherry, 272
Plums, Dried with Chicken and Green Olives, 135
Polenta, soft, 114
popcorn
    Home-Popped Kettle Corn, 80
pork
    Meatloaf, 129
    Ribs with Chuck's Barbecue Sauce, 158
potatoes. See also sweet potatoes
    Cabbage and Mashed Yukon Gold Potatoes, 110
    Cheesy Potato Casserole with Grilled Sausages, 38
    Shredded Potato Cake, 111
Pound Cake, Double Vanilla, 176
Preserves
    All-Season Tomato Sauce, 247
    Black and Blue Jam, 238
    Chili Sauce with Fruit, 248
    Crab Apple Jelly, 240
    Homemade Pizza Sauce, 246
    Peach Freezer Jam, 239
    Pear-Cranberry Chutney, 244
    Preserves and Pantry Items, 232
    Pickled Green Beans, 249
    Red and Black Jam, 237
    Strawberry-Vanilla Freezer Jam, 234
    Two-Burner Raspberry Jam, 243
Pretzel Caramels, 89
Prosciutto-Feta Bites, 107

puddings
    Chocolate Pudding, 87
    Jammy Bread Pudding, 33
    Steamed Carrot Pudding, 212
    Sweet Breakfast Custards, 9
    Vanilla Bean Tapioca Pudding, 88
Puffy Apple Pancake, 26
pumpkin
    Overnight Pumpkin Waffles, 34
    Pumpkin Cheesecake, 203
    Roasted Pumpkin Seeds, 78

Q
Quick Fried Rice, 53
Quiche, Asparagus and Ham, 41
quinoa
    Ginger Quinoa Granola, 6
    Quinoa Flakes, 6
    Quinoa Salad with Roasted Veggies, 45

R
Ranger Cookies, 81
Rarebit, Pimento-Cheese Welsh, 72
raspberries
    Raspberry Cream Cheese Brownie Ice Cream, 211
    Raspberry Cream Cheese Brownies, 179
    Red and Black Jam, 237
    Two-Burner Raspberry Jam, 243
    White Chocolate Raspberry Yule Log, 204
Red and Black Jam, 237
Red Onion, and Cheddar Biscuits, 27
Retro Cheese Ball, 102
rhubarb
    Rhubarb Gin and Tonic, 260
    Rhubarb Orange Blossom Syrup, 259
    Rhubarb-Vanilla Soda, 259
    Rosy Rhubarb Syrup, 259
    Strawberry Rhubarb Ice Pops, 86
Ribs with Chuck's Barbecue Sauce, 158
rice
    Chicken Soup with Rice, 48
    Quick Fried Rice, 53
    Watsa's Rice Pilau, 115

Risotto, Mixed Mushroom, 144
Roasted Pumpkin Seeds, 78
Roasted Veggies, Quinoa Salad with, 45
Rosy Rhubarb Syrup, 259

S
Sailboat Chicken, 140
salads. See also dressings & vinaigrettes
    Fresh Corn and Cherry Tomato Salad, 47
    Green Pea Salad with Mint And Goat Cheese, 64
    Grilled Chicken and Double Smoked Bacon Salad, 61
    Kale Tabbouleh, 67
    Quinoa Salad with Roasted Veggies, 45
    Romaine Salad with Creamy Italian Dressing and Fresh Garlic Croutons, 62
    Summer Bean Salad, 44
Saltine Crackers, 167
Salty Watercolours, 271
San Marzano Tomatoes, 247
sandwiches
    Dagwood Sandwiches, 54
    Grilled Pimento-Cheese Sandwiches, 72
    Lavender Shortbread Jam Sandwiches, 83
    Pimento-Cheese Welsh Rarebit, 72
sauces. See also condiments
    All-Season Tomato Sauce, 247
    Chili Sauce with Fruit, 248
    Homemade Pizza Sauce, 246
    Slow-Cooker Chili Sauce, 248
sausages
    Cheesy Potato Casserole with Grilled Sausages, 38
    Turkey Sausage Patties, 37
Scones, White Chocolate Apricot, 29
Senduk, Maurice, 48
Sesame Bread Sticks, Fresh, 105
Shanks Lamb, Braised, 160
Shirred Eggs with Maple Bacon, 23
Shortcakes, Strawberry, 174
Shrimp-in-a-Basket, 166

side dishes
    Baked Carrots with Horseradish, 123
    Broccoli with Cheddar Cheese
        Sauce, 125
    Cabbage and Mashed Yukon Gold
        Potatoes, 110
    Corn on the Cob with Roasted
        Tomato Butter, 118
    Cucumbers in Yogurt, 116
    Oven-Roasted Sweet Potato
        Wedges with Watercress Dip, 113
    Pan-Fried Brussels Sprouts with
        Maple Syrup and Bacon, 121
    Roasted Cauliflower, 122
    Soda Bread with Dried Cherries, 117
    Soft Polenta, 114
    Watsa's Rice Pilau, 115
Slow-Cooker Chili Sauce, 248
snacks
    Animal Crackers, 84
    Chocolate Pudding, 87
    Home-Popped Kettle Corn, 80
    Lavender Shortbread Jam
        Sandwiches, 83
    Pretzel Caramels, 89
    Peanut Butter Chocolate Squares,
        91
    Ranger Cookies, 81
    Roasted Pumpkin Seeds, 78
    Spotted Animal Crackers, 84
    Strawberry Ice Pops, 86
    Vanilla Bean Tapioca Pudding, 88
Soda, Rhubarb-Vanilla, 259
Soda Bread with Dried Cherries, 117
Soft Polenta, 114
soups
    Alphabet Soup, 50
    Broccoli-Cheddar Soup, 70
    Chicken Soup With Rice, 48
    Chicken Stock, 251
    Curried Coconut Chicken Soup,
        68
    Lentil and Carrot Soup, 52
    Veggie Stock, 252
Sour Cream Coffee Cake,
    Old-Fashioned, 30
Soy-Basted Roast Chicken, 165
Sparkling Clementine, 261
Spices, about, 138

spinach
    Cheesy Spinach and Apple
        Squares, 106
Spotted Animal Crackers, 84
squares. *See also* cookies
    Cheesy Spinach and Apple
        Squares, 106
    Peanut Butter Chocolate Squares,
        91
    Raspberry Cream Cheese
        Brownies, 179
Stamp, Cookie, 187
Stamped Shortbread Cookies, 187
starters. *See* appetizers
Steamed Carrot Pudding, 212
stock. *See also* Soup
    Chicken Stock, 251
    Veggie Stock, 252
strawberries
    Strawberry Oatmeal Muffins, 16
    Strawberry Ice Pops, 86
    Strawberry Rhubarb Ice Pops, 86
    Strawberry Shortcakes, 174
    Strawberry-Vanilla Freezer Jam,
        234
Stroganoff, Beef, 128
Strudel, Apple, 191
Stuffed Shells, 169
Sugared Violet Blossoms, 202
Summer Bean Salad, 44
Sunday Roast Beef Tenderloin, 152
Sweet Breakfast Custards, 9
sweet corn. *See* corn
sweet potatoes. *See also* potatoes
    Oven-Roasted Sweet Potato
        Wedges with Watercress Dip,
        113
    Sweet Potato and Zucchini Bread,
        32
    Sweet Potato Pie, 226
syrup
    Rhubarb Orange Blossom Syrup,
        259
    Rhubarb-Vanilla Syrup, 259
    Rosy Rhubarb Syrup, 259

T

Tabbouleh, Kale, 67
Tapioca, Vanilla Bean Pudding, 88

Tartar Sauce, 168
tarts
    Tomato Hand Tarts, 56
tea
    Barry's Irish Tea, 265
    Chai Tea, 265
Toast, Cinnamon Butter on, 12
Toast Shapes, Egg Cups and, 20
tomatoes
    All-Season Tomato Sauce, 247
    Corn on the Cob with Roasted
        Tomato Butter, 118
    Fresh Corn And Cherry Tomato
        Salad, 47
    Tomato Hand Tarts, 56
    White Bean and Tomato Linguini,
        145
    Turkey Sausage Patties, 37
Two-Burner Raspberry Jam, 243

U

V

vanilla and vanilla beans
    Double Vanilla Pound Cake,
        176
    Rhubarb-Vanilla Soda, 259
    Strawberry-Vanilla Freezer Jam, 234
    Vanilla Bean Tapioca Pudding, 88
    Vanilla Extract, 88
    Vanilla Marshmallows, 263
Veggie Cream Cheese on Bagels, 13
Veggie Stock, 252
Vermouth, about, 135
Very Cherry Play Dough, 272
vinaigrettes. *See* dressings and
    vinaigrettes; salads
Violet Cupcakes, 200
Violet Blossoms, Sugared, 202
vodka
    Orangeade, 256
    Vanilla Bean in Vodka, 88

W

waffles
    Overnight Pumpkin Waffles, 34
walnuts
    Cherry Crumble Oatmeal, 8
    Walnut-Spice Icebox Cookies, 185

Warm Olives, 95

Watercolours, Salty, 271

Watsa's Rice Pilau, 115

white chocolate

    White Chocolate Apricot Scones,
      29

    White Chocolate Raspberry Yule
      Log, 204

Wild Blueberries, 227

Winter Meat Pies, 156

Y

yogurt

    Cucumbers in Yogurt, 116

    Homemade Yogurt, About, 7

    Lamb Burgers with Yogurt-
      Cucumber Spread, 132

Yule Log, White Chocolate
      Raspberry, 204

Z

zucchini

    Sweet Potato and Zucchini Bread,
      32